CHARACTER

Tracy,

Thank you so much for your support. Best wishes in all your endeavors.

God bless,

Kate M. L.

CHARACTER

◆

Becoming the Real You, By Knowing Your True Character

Debut self-help book from motivational speaker
Keke M. Robinson
President/CEO of Character Consulting Services

iUniverse, Inc.
New York Lincoln Shanghai

CHARACTER
Becoming the Real You, By Knowing Your True Character

Copyright © 2005 by Keke M. Robinson

All rights reserved. No part of this book may be used or reproduced by any means, graphic, electronic, or mechanical, including photocopying, recording, taping or by any information storage retrieval system without the written permission of the publisher except in the case of brief quotations embodied in critical articles and reviews.

iUniverse books may be ordered through booksellers or by contacting:

iUniverse
2021 Pine Lake Road, Suite 100
Lincoln, NE 68512
www.iuniverse.com
1-800-Authors (1-800-288-4677)

All scripture quotations, unless otherwise indicated, are taken from the New King James Version. Copyright 1982 by Thomas Nelson, Inc. Used by permission. All rights reserved.

All definitions are taken from the Webster Dictionary and Thesaurus, Deluxe Edition. Copyright 2001 by V. Nichols. Used by permission.

ISBN: 0-595-32780-X

Printed in the United States of America

DEDICATIONS

I DEDICATE THIS BOOK TO MY LORD AND SAVIOUR. JESUS CHRIST HAS BROUGHT ME THROUGH AND IS BRINGING ME THROUGH MY TRIALS AND TRIBULATIONS AND HE IS NOT THROUGH WITH ME YET!

THANK YOU

I THANK MY CHILDREN. KIERA, TIA, JULIANA, AKILIA, AND STEDMON. THEY HAVE BEEN MY LITTLE SOLDIERS, MY BLESSINGS, MY ROCK, AND MY STRENGTH. I LOVE YOU VERY, VERY MUCH.

I THANK MY PARENTS; MY MOTHER, GEORGIA GREEN. THANK YOU SO MUCH FOR YOUR SUPPORT AND LOVE.

MY FATHER, WALLACE GUIDRY, THANK YOU SO MUCH FOR YOUR UNCONDITIONAL LOVE, NEVER-ENDING SUPPORT, ENCOURAGEMENT, AND BELIEF IN ME. YOU ARE MY ROCK. YOU HAVE MADE MY DREAMS POSSIBLE.

I THANK MY BEST FRIEND; MY SISTER, BERNESTER DUPREE. YOU HAVE BEEN MY CHEERLEADER, MY SUPPORT SYSTEM. I AM OPENING THE DOOR SO THAT YOU AND OTHERS WILL BE ABLE TO FOLLOW.

I THANK BISHOP T.D. JAKES AND BISHOP NOEL JONES MINISTRIES. POWERFUL, POWERFUL MEN OF GOD. UNBEKNOWNST YOU, YOUR MINISTRIES HAVE CHANGED MY LIFE.

I THANK ALL THE PEOPLE WHOM HAVE CROSSED MY PATH OVER THE YEARS AND ENCOURAGED AND INSPIRED ME IN ONE WAY OR ANOTHER.

Contents

INTRODUCTION ix

CHAPTER 1 LEARNING THE ASPECTS OF YOUR
CHARACTER 1

CHAPTER 2 THE 4 DEPARTMENTS OF YOUR
CHARACTER 12

CHAPTER 3 ARE YOU GIVING MORE THAN YOU ARE
RECEIVING? 24

CHAPTER 4 BATTLE SCARS: MAKING IT THROUGH
THE PAIN 43

CHAPTER 5 FOUNDATION: BUILDING ON SOLID
GROUND 56

CHAPTER 6 FINALLY! BECOMING THE 'REAL' ME 70

CHARACTER SCRIPTURES 85

CHARACTER DEFINITIONS 101

ABOUT THE AUTHOR 117

INTRODUCTION

Everyone has something about him or her that defines him or her as a person. That personal identifying trait is what illuminates their persona. Everyone should have the 'Character' trait. Your Character makes you distinctive from anyone else. Your Character is your true identity. It's about being the 'real' you at all times. Being the 'real' you even when no one is looking.

I have been guilty of losing my identity. I have repressed dramatic situations that have happened to me in my childhood. I have spent over twelve years in unfulfilling and abusive relationships. I have had children out of wedlock and have had to cope with the guilt of putting my child up for adoption.

I have struggled with bouts of depression, low self-esteem and low self-worth. I have had to deal with the fear that I would never get it right. I was afraid that it would be too late for me to discover my true self. I had to be truly broken and the grace of God had to come in and restore me. HE had to make me whole.

If you or anyone you know of had to go through any painful struggles, this book will encourage, motivate, and liberate you to continue on your journey to self-discovery. There *is* a light at the end of the dark tunnel.

If you quit now, you will never know "what could have been." God has a plan for each and everyone of us.

When you have true character, you have control over your life. You are able to release things that you do not need anymore. You are able to refrain from unhealthy situations. I pray that this book helps you find the grace that is within your person. CHARACTER should help you search the inner depths of your soul, reassess your life, get the necessary tools to rebuild your foundation, and discover the REAL you.

I have included exercises, key-term definitions, 8 necessities to protect yourself against life's storms, and powerful scriptures from the King James Holy Bible to assist you with your Character transformation.

My goal in writing this book is to share my own personal experiences and my research to help you discover the answer to the question, "WHO AM I REALLY?" Prayerfully, after reading this book you will be able to answer, "I AM............"

"REMEMBER, IT IS IMPORTANT TO HAVE CHARACTER AND NOT JUST BE A CHARACTER."

Allow yourself to undergo a *metamorphosis*.

Meta—change   **Morphosis**—form   Allow your whole form to change.

C-HANGE

H-APPINESS

A-LWAYS LOVE YOURSELF

R-EAL

A-LLOWING 'YOU', TO BE YOU

C-HOICES

T-RUST YOUR INTUITION

E-AGER TO ACHIEVE

R-EBUILDING YOUR LIFE

1

Learning the Aspects of Your Character

In order to truly learn the aspects of your Character, you need to do a self-evaluation. You need to be able to ask yourself a series of simple questions and evaluate your honest answers. You possess the power within you to change your life. Let's take this simple self-evaluation:

HONESTLY ANSWER THESE QUESTIONS. AS OF TODAY;

1. **WHO AM I?**

2. **WHAT TRAITS MAKE UP MY CHARACTER?**

3. **IF I COULD CHANGE ANYTHING ABOUT MY CHARACTER, I WOULD CHANGE.........**

CHAPTER 1
"LEARNING THE ASPECTS OF YOUR CHARACTER"

"YOUR CHARACTER'S MAKE-UP"

Your Character is about distinctively being who you really are at all times. Everything we do, everyone that we encounter, every environment that we come in contact with plays a part in building our Character. What we instill and allow to be instilled into our spirit, soul, body, and mind lays the foundation of our person. It adds layers onto our development.

A layer of knowledge, trust, honesty, integrity, or a layer of low self-esteem, issues, or baggage can come from our contacts. Our intake becomes a part of our make-up.

That make-up ultimately defines who we are. Our Character. That is why it is so important to monitor what we are feeding our souls. We must not allow toxics to enter in and pollute our beings. What we intake and digest on the inside has to have a release and eventually is projected on the outside.

For example, if we eat too much, what foods we take in on the inside will eventually show itself as weight gain on the outside. If our thoughts of ourselves are negative and filled with unworthiness, combined with low self-esteem, then it will show itself as being timid, intimidation, withdrawal, and/or being anti-social on the outside. What is on the inside, whether positive or negative, will manifest itself on the outside. This process can work both ways. What we are exposed to on the outside in our environment, whether positive or negative, can influence who we are, our structure on the inside.

Some results may be hereditary or may be the end product of our environment. Either way, if it is not for your good, you can change that, by discovering your true Character. You have to come into the acknowledgement of who you are. You have to discover your value, your worth, your capabilities and your purpose in this life. You do not need to know someone else's purpose for your life. You need to know God's purpose for your life.

Assess who you are right now. Ask yourself, "Is this the real me?" Or is it a combination of your parents, your siblings, your friends, your pastor's wife, your favorite celebrity? Is this the real you or are you imitating someone else's life? Do not be exposed as a fraud. Who are you really? Will the 'real you' please stand up.

During my childhood, I have always been very wise for my age. My elders would say that I was very "grown." I did not catch up with myself until I was in my mid-twenties and had suffered through many different, life-changing experiences. Some experiences were good. They helped me to mature, to catch up with my "grown" self. Those experiences showed me how to love, to have patience, grace, and to have an unwavering faith in my Lord.

Some experiences were bad. They also helped me to catch up with my "grown" self, to mature, to have patience, grace, and have an unwavering faith in my Lord, also. Life is an unbiased teacher. It does not discriminate. It can make you or it can break you, but either way you will end up learning something about yourself. My suggestion to you is, when life throws you lemons, get out your pitcher, water, ice, and a little sugar and make yourself a tall, cool, sweet glass of lemonade. Drink up and enjoy.

"LIFE'S TESTS"

I have been raped, abused, had failed relationships, and have had five children out-of-wedlock. All of these experiences in my life were NECESSARY. They were all necessary. No matter, what I have been through, each situation were necessary tools to create who I am and who I am becoming. My *Life Tests* are my testimony on receiving passing grades on the development of my Character.

Everything we achieve in life comes through a test. Our whole system as citizens consists of tests. Education is essentially all tests. Each grade level brings a new test, to cover what you should have learned. If you pass that grade's series of tests then you are now qualified to advance to the next grade. To receive a driver's license, we had to take a driver's test. Sometimes to become employed we have to take and pass a drug test.

Our whole life consists of tests to be taken and passed so that we may advance to the next level. These achievements say that we are qualified to be in the positions that we currently hold. You can say my Character is who I am because of the experiences that I have been through. I have been tested and I have passed that test. I am Qualified to be Who I Am. Have you received a passing grade on your Character or are you cheating off someone else's passing grade on their Character?

"WHO ARE YOU, REALLY?"

Do you feel like, it is too painful to be the real you? Is it easier to be someone else? Is it easier, perhaps possibly safer to become fulfilled by hiding in another person's shadow? You have to step out from behind that shadow and shine in your own light. Everyone has potential, but potential is only good if you do something with it. Everyone has a purpose.

You have to discover what is your purpose. You have to find out what is your destiny. What legacy would you like to leave behind? But before you can do any of that you have to find out who you really are.

Let's get one thing straight, who you are is not your title. You may have a high-powered position, but that is not *who* you are, that is *what* you do! We as women have to find out who we are. And defining who we are is not by the things that we do. We cover up our lack of fulfillment, by constantly hiding behind the roles that we play. You have to pull back the layers and *look* inside, then *go* inside of yourself. Start at the very bottom, your foundation, and work your way up. You need to identify yourself to yourself.

Your title is not who you are. You can be a schoolteacher, bus driver, cashier, volunteer, singer, stay-at-home mom, actor, or even CEO of a corporation, but that is not who you are, that is what you do. You cannot assert yourself to others because you do not truly know yourself. You are living behind your title and that is how others will begin to recognize you. "That's Leroy's wife"; "Hey, Mrs. Smith, my 5th grade teacher"; "I don't remember her name, but she works at a Fortune 500 corporation"; "She plays Joan on that television show"; "Isn't that Pookie's mother?"

Sure, that may all be true, but after being Pookie's mama, who are you? Better yet, who were you before you became Pookie's mama? What would happen if all your titles were gone? If all your titles were stripped away, who are you? If you do not know the answer to this question, then please do not be caught exposed naked to the world without your title. Your Character goes beyond your title(s). You have to realize who you are.

"SPEND TIME ALONE"

Honestly answer these questions: What goals wake you up everyday? What are you aiming to accomplish? At the end of your day are you satisfied? Ask yourself these questions and answer them honestly. You have to begin the process of evolving into your true Character. It is never too late to embark on your journey to self-discovery. There is no such thing as failure...and giving up is not an option.

You have to realize that you are not a mistake, as humans we make mistakes. Sometimes we have to go through trial and error to discover our identity. If you truly allow your metamorphosis to begin, you will always learn something new about yourself.

We can respect and admire others. We can have role models. But **you** should be the most interesting person that you know (or at least one of them). You should be able to focus when interacting with others. Your Character should display honesty, integrity, confidence, and self-control. You should not appear empty-hearted, empty-handed, or empty-headed. You should be able to enjoy spending time with yourself. There is always something to learn about you. Never confuse being alone with being lonely.

"YOU NEED TO REST"

Learn to become one with yourself: spiritually, physically, emotionally, and mentally. You can put these areas in the order that best suits you. Get in touch with these areas, but most importantly learn to REST. To help develop or redevelop your Character is to have a good support network of your faith, your family, and good friends. But above all else you need to have REST.

You have to take the time to rejuvenate. When you are cleansing your soul and getting spiritually in tuned with your mind, your whole being, you need rest. Complete rest. You need to relinquish anyone or anything that has put restraints on you and your life. You need to be able to relive any positive influences that have contribute to your growth.

You should be able to go through the reliance of trusting your Character instincts. Cry if you need to, to release and rid your body of any pollutants that need to come out. A good cry can always help you shed unwanted issues. Once you had that cry, it is OVER! Do not dwell on that particular situation ever again. Release it, cut it, loose it and let it go.

Here is an exercise, you can perform if you want to release any negativity within your being:

Make sure that you are in a nice, calm, quiet, and isolated place where you can have alone time with yourself. Get naked. Taking off each layer of clothing is being symbolic of shedding unwanted layers of your life. Find a place to lie down and do so. Just lay still...meditate...have an out-of-body experience as you are becoming one with yourself. Give yourself permission to shed all the negative traits that are in your Character. Give yourself the freedom to become…Reborn.

You are brand new. Make rest apart of your life. You need intervals where you can get refreshed, become rejuvenated, to revive your being. You can voluntary take a break or involuntarily become broken. You have to take care of you, before you can fully be effective in any other area of your life.

Even the Lord had to rest. He made the world in 6 days and on the 7th day He rested. The 8th is a symbol of new beginnings. This is your new beginning to the new you, your new Character, but you need to include rest.

When you get renewed, those things that use to make you cry, bitter, frustrated, or irritable can now make you laugh. They definitely will do not possess the same impact that they once had. Happy people, fresh people, real people, a 'renewed' person is attractive. When your spirit is right, you will attract positive people to you. If others come along, that do not align with your spirit, you will be able to recognize that. Being renewed, helps you to be aware of your surroundings.

"FINE-TUNING OUR MAGNETS"

Have you ever heard of the expression "tired of being sick and tired"? Well, this expression goes beyond being physically tired. It relates to being tired in those main areas of your life. The areas of being *spiritually, mentally, emotionally,* and *physically* tired. When you are tired, you can sometimes make regretful decisions, because you are not at your best. When we allow our Character, our being to be affected by our environment, our foundation is weakened. Our levels are flawed and our judgments are cloudy.

Our Character traits attract certain types of people in our life. For example, if married men are always trying to pick you up, there is something wrong. There is something inside of you that keep attracting those types of pursuers. For married men to even have the audacity to think that you wouldn't mind being the other woman is unacceptable. I am not talking about those once or twice occurrences. You can chalk those up to coincidences, but if these approaches occur on a regular basis then you need to do a self-evaluation. There is a 'magnet' in our Character. The charisma that outlines our persona naturally attracts whomever or whatever. You can be in a room with over 500 people, but you could find possibly 5 people that you just 'click' with. It is your 'magnet' that draws you to your peers or draws your peers to you. And I will say again that it can be positive or negative.

You need to go within your inner being to dissect the old adage phrase, 'birds of a feather, flock together'. You hang around the people that you like or want to be like. The question now is, does these people contribute the necessary attributes to your Character? You have to stop trying to get people to like you. You do not know how you are going to feel today, until you see how someone else is going to feel. When you keep trying to align your feelings and spirit up with someone else, it is just not going to fit. The puzzle piece doesn't fit because the piece has square corners, but your Character needs a rounded corner piece. It will not fit.

You have to have your spirit purged and cleanse, to become aligned with your soul. It is all connected. Our depth depends on it. The deeper we go into our soul, the higher up we can excel in life. In the process of finding out how life works, our destination, *who* we really are and most importantly, *whose* we are in Christ.

We are now in process of developing/redeveloping our Character. We have to learn to take the magnets out of our being, deactivate them, so we will not attract the wrong people or things into our lives. We have to literally turn ourselves inside out. We have to begin to the process by cleansing, repenting, rediscovering, redeveloping, nurturing, and absolutely loving ourselves. You have to go from being transparent to being transitioned.

"TRANSFORMATION"

You are now being transformed into your new Character. When you get rid of the old baggage, the trash, the fine grains of grit that was left on you, people should not be able to recognize you.

Oh, they will know you, because your features will not change. But the beauty of your new 'after glow' will make you unrecognizable. Your positive attitude about yourself and life will abundantly shine through you. You will not have to say a word. Your mere presence will shout your story. You can begin to accept who you really are. When you are ready to have relations with others, then you put your magnet back in, and just wait and see the positive people and things that you will attract to you.

The old crowd, will not even approach you, because your strong aura will say "I don't think so, don't even try it!" Knowing who you are will not allow access to manipulation, intimidation, or slackers into your life.

HONESTLY ANSWER THESE QUESTIONS;

1. What makes you get up everyday?

2. What goal(s) have you set for yourself?

3. At this very moment, what are you aiming to achieve?

4. At the end of your day, are you satisfied with your accomplishments?

5. What could you do better or differently?

6. Are you ready to take the necessary steps to become the 'real you'?

WHAT ARE YOUR THOUGHTS ABOUT CHAPTER 1?

WHAT HAVE YOU LEARNED FROM CHAPTER 1?

WHAT NECESSARY CHANGES CAN YOU MAKE IN YOUR CHARACTER, FROM THE KNOWLEDGE THAT YOU HAVE GAINED FROM CHAPTER 1?

2

The 4 Departments of Your Character

You have to be able to determine what makes you, the person you are. You have to be able to set your priorities ahead of anyone and anything else. Determining the four departments that makes up your Character, allows you to see the whole picture and evaluate the elements that you deemed important enough to make you complete.

Honestly answer the following questions:

1. **How would you define your personality?**

2. **What are your main priorities?**

3. **Everyday you must do…….**

4. **What are the people/things that you can/cannot do without?**

5. **When you combine all of your answers, does this define who you are?**

6. **Why or why not?**

Chapter 2
Your Four Departments that Help Make Up Your Character

"CONTRIBUTIONS TO YOUR CHARACTER"

Your Character is about being who you really are. Being the 'real you' at all times. Everything we do and say to others and ourselves plays a role in the development of our Character. Because we have daily interactions with our environment, something is always being added to or taken away from our Character. A lot of the times it is being done without our knowledge. Sometimes we are not even aware of the elements that contribute to the development of our Character when it is actually happening. Different elements may manifest within us, but lay dormant. We may be unaware of its very existence until one day out of the blue, it just shows up and we are like, "Whoa! Where did that come from?" You are absolutely clueless that it has been within you all along. Ask yourself these questions: Who am I? Who am I today? Is it possible for you to be a different person today than on yesterday? Well, physically, by natural accounts, no it is not possible. But emotionally, mentally, and spiritually…yes, it is possible.

We all have different personalities that we combine to make one individual. We each have four, special departments that help make up our persona. Let's do an exercise, to help see what are your four main departments. This exercise will help you prioritize what your main departments are or what they should be. And what are the compartments that you have in these departments.

Divide yourself into 4 parts and label each section. Each section represents a part of your being. The combination of all 4 parts helps to make up your whole person. For example;

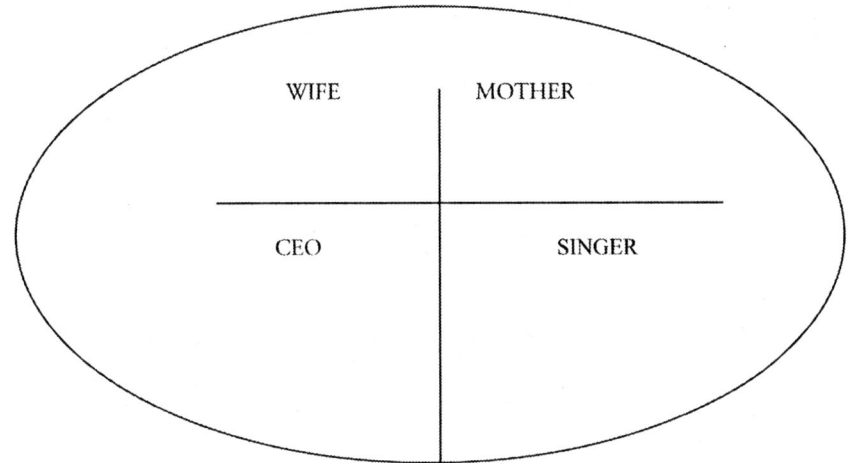

Your four main departments that makes up your persona, your Character.

"DEPARTMENTS VS. COMPARTMENTS"

The four sections should be labeled according to what is important to you. This is however you see yourself. Then everything else is branched out from these sections. We are only doing only 4 sections, because we do not want to over indulge. Giving 25% to each section can allow for a balance, rather than creating a strain to give yourself to everything, but never fully completing anything.

There should not be too many "MUST-HAVE" priorities in your life. Some "MUST-HAVE" priorities that you have as departments should really be compartments in your life. Compartments are still very important, but they are not the whole picture. Compartments are important to the development of your persona, your Character, but they do not carry enough weight to make up your complete person by itself.

Let's use a symbolic example; your purse is a major department. It is very important. The small, zipped compartment inside the purse is also very important. You can use the small compartment to hold your credit cards, cash, lipstick or gum. The compartment is a very useful amenity, but it is not the whole purse. So even though the compartment is certainly helpful, if the purse did not have it you will still be able to manage.

Now, let's evaluate each of your departments along with, if any, their compartments. What do you give to each section? What do you receive from each section? Now, let's decide why is each section important to you, why are they a priority?

These questions are to help you assess the inflows and outflows of your life.

Does your assessment meet your approval?

Why or why not?

Do you need to make any changes?

What changes are necessary?

What could be a priority that wasn't one before?

What does not need to be a priority anymore?

Do you need to go in and adjust a few things?

"YOU NEED BALANCE"

To learn what traits make up your Character. You need to know yourself. When I began to rebuild my Character, I needed to get to know me. I had to strip myself of all outside influences that help develop in the molding of my Character and get down to the bare essentials. After getting my foundation right, I was ready to build on solid ground. Well, I basically had to spend some intimate time alone with myself.

I had to learn that I was able to rely on myself. I was dependable for others; I needed to be dependable for ME. I had to learn to trust my own intuition. Others may be able to see things about you that you are unable to see. I had to find out the things about myself that I wanted to accept and the things that I wanted to remove from my Character.

When you make the decision to recondition your mind, you must recondition your body. It is a combination process in order to function properly. Your mind, body, soul, **and** spirit need to be conditioned. To function properly each area has to be taken care of and balanced. Your whole package needs to be conditioned. Just like you have 4 departments to make up your Character, you have 4 departments to make up your inner being.

Physical, mental, spiritual, and emotional are the 4 departments that make up your inner being. To have a complete balance, all departments must be balanced.

If one department isn't being fulfilled, or isn't working properly, it throws the other departments off track. There is no exception. There must be a balance.

"EVALUATE YOURSELF"

When you recondition your being, you must recondition every area properly. Each area must receive its proper nourishment to function properly, so you can therefore led a balanced life. The new you, the 'real you' can and will be whole.

Your wholeness is key. Half-people attract other half-people. (Remember, we discussed the fact that we have a 'magnet' within us in Chapter 1.) Half-people look to others for their fulfillment and when it becomes a burden to the other person to keep you 'up' all the time, then you get angry. It can work both ways. If you have to keep the other person 'up' all the time, you may become angry.

Being whole means *to be without lack; complete.* When you are a half-person, you become a burden, to others, and even more so to yourself. You become a liability. When you are whole, complete or without lack you are an asset. You are a positive addition.

You need to make your Characteristic traits personal. By being personal, I mean, your Character is something distinctive about you. You need to make sure that what you possess within you, belongs to you. You possess a natural quality that belongs to you and not anyone else.

This may seem like a long drawn out process, but actually it is not. If you do not let yourself become overwhelmed, you can overcome any obstacle that may stand in the way of your destination. Getting your foundation together may be the most difficult, but worthwhile, process. The building should be the fun part.

Let's do an honest assessment of yourself. Ask yourself the following questions:

What defines Me?

What do I think of Myself?

What do I think of my "Private Self"?

What do I think of my "Public Self"?

Are there any changes I would like to make?

Why or Why Not?

How can I go about making the necessary changes?

How will my life be different with these changes?

Make a list of everything that you **like** about yourself. For example, start with your outward being and work your way inward.

- **Do you like your eyes?**
- **Do you like your hair?**
- **Do you like your smile?**
- **Do you like that you are a "people" person?**
- **Do you like being alone?**
- **Do you like being sensitive?**
- **Do you like being a no nonsense person?**

Make a list of the things that you **do not like** about yourself. For example, start with your outward being and work your way inward.

- **I dislike that I am a "people" pleaser.**
- **I dislike that I am too short.**
- **I dislike that I am too tall.**
- **I dislike that I am a pushover.**
- **I dislike that I am a bully.**
- **I dislike that I am too sensitive.**
- **I dislike that I cannot say No.**

You need to decide what necessary steps that you are going to take to begin your Character "overhaul" process. Analyze what you can change and what you cannot change about yourself. Now, remember that you need to give yourself a reasonable amount of time to make changes. It is all about seeing the progress. You do not have to try the "sink or swim" method all at once, but it is also important not to stall. You do not need to keep putting off your process for a 'better' time nor do you need to rush in and try to 'revamp' yourself overnight. Rushing your progress can result in a setback. You need to allow yourself enough time to go through the proper procedure.

One more powerful question, you should ask yourself and answer honestly, **When you hear your name, what is the first thing that you think of?** That very answer may help you build on the platform of what defines you. I asked a lady that very question. We were trying to discover what defined her. I asked her what was the first thing that came to mind when I said her name. She answered her husband. Take your answer and analyze why that is your answer.

You have to come into the acknowledgement of who you are. You need to know your value, your worth, your capabilities, and your limitations.

WHAT ARE YOUR 4 DEPARTMENTS?

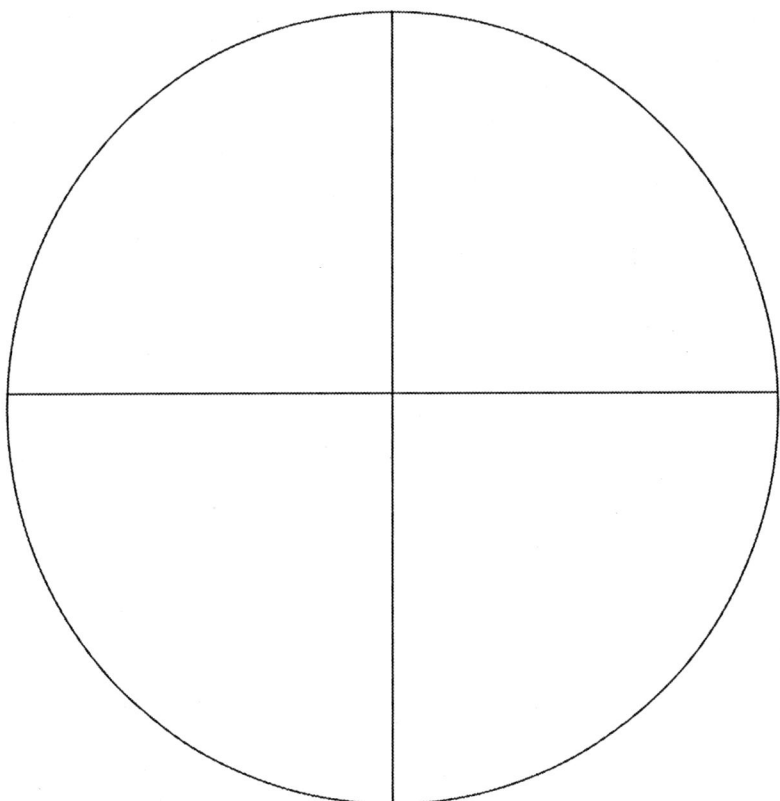

List your four departments and, if any, compartments.
Do you need to reprioritize?

1. **If you could take one of the four departments out of the equation, which one would you eliminate?**

2. **Why would you make that change?**

3. **If you could add a department in place of the one that you eliminated, what would that be?**

4. **Why would you make *that* change?**

WHAT ARE YOUR THOUGHTS ABOUT CHAPTER 2?

WHAT HAVE YOU LEARNED FROM CHAPTER 2?

WHAT NECESSARY CHANGES CAN YOU MAKE IN YOUR CHARACTER, FROM THE KNOWLEDGE THAT YOU GAINED FROM CHAPTER 2?

3

Are You Giving More Than You Are Receiving?

"DEFINING YOUR ROLES"

1. How many different roles do you play? (For an example; are you a mother, wife, student, secretary, CEO, or a volunteer, etc.?)

2. How often do you contribute to these roles? Daily, weekly, biweekly, monthly, annually?

3. Are these roles too time consuming?

4. Are you doing so much that your efforts yield mediocre results.

5. Could these tasks continue on without you?

6. Could you do your best in other areas of importance if you eliminate some of these unnecessary areas?

7. Could you delete any one these areas and still feel good about yourself?

8. Are you contributing to these roles for private or public glory?

9. What are you receiving in return?

10. Is it a fair exchange?

Chapter 3
Are you giving more than you are receiving?

"FEED YOUR SOUL"

How many hats do you wear? Do you play so many roles that sometimes you lose count? So many of us are guilty of always overloading ourselves. We are literally weighed down with our issues, and then we take on other people's issues. We cannot get in touch with our Character, because we are constantly dealing with everyone else's problems. Or it may not be someone it could be something.

Have you ever heard someone say, "If it isn't one thing, it is another?" Well, it doesn't have to be that way, unless *you* let it be that way. I am speaking of the things in which you have control over. Do you know someone who is always on the go, even if there is no reason for them to be in such a hurry? It is almost like, if they are not busy, then they are not happy. I know people like that and I have told them to STOP!

Be still and take a time out. Sit down while you can before you have to lie down when you do not want to. Meaning, before you end up sick and in the hospital or even worse, dead in a morgue.

I use to wonder about "busy bodies". They have to have their hands into anything and everything. Then I realized, most of these people hate spending time alone. It is something about themselves that they do not want to deal with. As long as they are constantly on the grind, they do not have to think about it.

Deep in their Character, they have some hidden secrets in the recesses of their mind that they do not want to face. It is the same for people who vicariously live through others. For example, parents whose children's lives become their lives. Maybe, you do not know anyone else like that. Maybe this describes *you*.

At some point in our lives, we all have been guilty of giving more than we have received. And a lot of times we do not become aware of it, until something drastic occurs. You may not be aware that you are running off of fumes until the whole car (*you*) breaks down. That is why you have to make sure that everything you do comes Full Circle. There must be a balance. There must be a Fair Exchange.

Now I am not talking about the roles that are priorities in your life, such as; wife, mother, or whatever priority role you have. But the key word is, *priority*. These roles should automatically feed your soul in return. We will develop clues to discover whether they do or not.

First of all, you have to know your Character. You have to know the 'real you', so therefore you will know your limitations. People do not know your limitations, because you train people how to treat you. They will continue to take from you as long as you continue to give. Seemly, you will continue to give as long as they continue to take. You want to feel needed. No matter how much of yourself you may lose in the process.

You feel like you do not mind giving so much because that is apart of your Character. Being a giver is one of your traits. Well, that is wonderful, but being a receiver needs to be one of your traits, also. Sometimes you can give so much to the people you love (and to some people you do not love) because you want them to be happy. You feel happy as long as they are happy. Or sometimes you feel that as long as they are happy, your feelings do not matter. You may just want to keep peace, either way this is dangerous territory for you.

"A BREWING TIMEBOMB"

When you harbor so many unreleased issues and you are not receiving a proper intake to match your outtake, implosive bombs are created. You have to be careful to whom and what you are giving yourself to. Some people are not going to be happy, unless you are miserable. They can see you in trouble, will stand by, watch you crash and burn and not even offer you water, that they have in their possession, to help put out your flames. That is why you cannot please everyone, because everyone is not going to want to see you happy.

That is why it is important to know who you are. What are your priorities, capabilities, and/or limitations? You have to make sure you are taken care of. You have to know and love yourself before you can share these necessities with someone else.

When you are trying to give out more than you even truly have, that implosive bomb is brewing inside, and you feel as if you are on the verge of a nervous breakdown.

- "Honey, could you iron my shirt?" "Sure."
  TICK TOCK
- "Mom, I need $50 to go to the mall." "Sure."
  TICK TOCK
- "I need you to drive the kids' carpool this month." "Sure."
  TICK TOCK

- "Baby, I need a cup a coffee, black." "Sure."

  TICK TOCK

- "I need you to work over tonight." "Sure."

  TICK TOCK

- "Could you bake 6 dozen cookies for the school's bake sale by tomorrow?" "Sure."

  TICK TOCK

You are grinning and bearing it, all the while you are down to seconds on your implosive bomb. Your implosive bomb is brewing so much that it is running over. It is silent to everyone. No one can hear it. Only you. The ticking is so loud, it is deafening in your ears. The ticking is so deafening that your vision is blurry, you are dizzy, and you are on the verge of a nosebleed.

No one knows this, because you have kept it all in. You do not want to disappoint anyone. "I am a Giver." "I am a Giver." "I may not get what I need in return, but that is okay because I am a Giver…"

So when the implosive bomb does explode from the inside out, it is such a shock to everyone. No one would have guessed that you could have gone off the way that you did. Who knew? That is why some women have been in the news in the recent years for killing their own children or their spouses. They are so remorseful after it happens. They cannot believe that it has happened, but it did happen. Their family and friends could not believe it. They would have never suspected that 'she' was capable of doing something so horrible.

But something so horrible is possible when you are carrying around an implosive bomb within you. When your implosive bomb is brewing on the inside and you do not seek the help that you need, your implosive bomb will explode on the outside for everyone to see. So, do not try to hold it in and keep it all together for others' sakes, because it will manifest and show itself in the worse way. You will blow up!

"TAKING CARE OF SELF"

Go to the Lord. Ask Him to expose you to *you*. Discover who you really are, what you really need and what is your purpose in this life. You have to take care of yourself. Have you heard the expression that, "there is no "I" in TEAM"? Well, that is true, but there *is* a "U" in YOU/YOURSELF". If you do not take care of *yourself* then you cannot be effective for the *team*. There is no I in TEAM, but there is a U in YOU/YOURSELF. If you are not at your best, then you cannot give your best.

"GETTING COMPENSATION FOR YOUR CONTRIBUTIONS"

When you give so much and never receive, you will eventually end up, tapped out. A bank is symbolic to your person. If you are constantly allowing withdrawals out of your account, without constantly receiving deposits, you will end up without any funds. You will be in the red. Your assets will all become liabilities, and you will eventually end up bankrupt.

Anything that you contribute to requires your time, energy, and sometimes your love and/or finance. Anyway that you contribute to an area, you are using one of these elements. The person or area that is worthwhile of your contribution should be replenishing to you in some way. In other words, any person or area you contribute to, you should receive something in return for your contribution.

I am not talking about just monetary. You can go to a job that you hate and receive money from it. You can expect to get paid for your services, but if you are giving your time, energy, and assistance and in return you only receive headaches, ulcers, a negative attitude…*and* money. Well, you may want to find another job or start your own business.

I will work this another way. Any positive contribution you give, you should be able to expect a positive reception in return. In order to survive, you must receive as much as you give. You have to be properly compensated for your contributions. There has to be a fair exchange. There must be a full circle, in order to create a balance.

When there is a fair exchange, your Character is balanced; therefore your life is balanced. When it comes to compensation for your contributions, there must not be any negotiations. Nothing or no one should be in your life if they contribute to clouding your judgment. You must possess a clear mind and make rational decisions.

"BARGAINING YOURSELF"

Do not bargain your needs. Do not bargain yourself. Who is willing to pay full price for something that is on sale? No one. Would you tell a sales clerk, "I know that this sweater is on sale for $50, but please let me pay the $100 regular price for it?" Of course you would not say that! You would pay that $50 and be ecstatic that you got such a great deal. You have gotten a bargain.

No one will be willing to pay whole price for you, if you keep putting yourself on sale. Baby, do not bargain yourself. You are worth more than that; in fact you are Priceless! And if you do not think so, neither will anyone else. That is why it is important to know your value, know your worth, and know yourself, because if not, you will be the one to end up getting shortchanged.

Sometimes we are so willing to put our Character on sale for our relationships, for our friends, for our jobs, etc. You should not do that. You must stop doing that. You are willing to commit so much of yourself to learning about other people, other things, and you know nothing about yourself. Well, I take that back, you do know that you are tired. You are tired of being the way you are. You are so tired because you do not have a balance in your life.

"GIVERS AND TAKERS"

You went from running on more than enough, to not quite enough, to barely nothing. Now you are kaput, and you have no backup plan. Do not allow yourself to become down and out. It is time to assess your receiving status. List all the areas that you contribute to and their compensations into your life. If you are giving more than you are receiving, it is time to start weeding out some of the 'extra fluff' areas in your life. Your diagram of your 4 departments can assist you in this exercise.

Sometimes, the process of weeding out can be hard. By nature we as women are nurturers. We are designed to be Givers (Givers of Life). But as Givers we must not be manipulated by Takers. We have to know and create a balance. Honestly, our sanity depends on it. I believe that all women can relate to this in one way or another.

"LIVING/HIDING BEHIND THE MASK"

You are in a 'perfect' marriage, you are a 'stay-at-home' mom, even though you love your family, but being there all day, everyday can become stifling, congested, and it can begin suffocating you if you never have time to yourself. You can end up feeling as if you are trapped in a box, clawing to get out, screaming at the top of your lungs, but no one hears your screams…but you, you are practically drowning in them.

You could be a 'corporate' woman. You have arrived! You are successful. You have achieved so many awards, accolades, gifts, recognition, and all the material amenities that comes with success. But at the end of the day, when you get into your Mercedes Benz and drive to your beautiful 10,000 square feet home, you are falling apart.

Tears begin to silently stream down your face, unnoticed. They have fallen on your silk Chanel blouse. You haven't realized that you had been crying until you parked your car in your driveway and take the key out of the ignition. You do not even give yourself time to collect your thoughts, your feelings, or even yourself.

You will not even allow yourself to register that there is an implosive bomb brewing inside of you. You just pat your face dry, compose yourself, and put the mask back on (that has obviously fallen off, not realizing that there are many cracks in it), to go inside and 'perform' your daily routine.

No one knows that both of these 'perfect' women, the stay-at-home mom and the CEO, are on the verge of a nervous breakdown. They both live very different lives and both seems to have it all together on the outside. They look fine to everyone on the outside, but unbeknownst to anyone, they are both deteriorating on the inside.

You do not have to be poor, rich, old, young, black, white, or Latino for your inner being to hurt. This is universal, it can and will affect anyone. The important thing is to be able to recognize the signs. If you are giving more than you are receiving, you are running off of fumes.

"YOU ARE # 1"

Everyone and everything needs maintenance. You will take your car in for a tune-up, but you will not 'tune-up' yourself. You know no one can take care of you like God. God has appointed each one of us as CEO over our own bodies. Sometimes you feel as if you do not have enough time in the day to accomplish everything you need to get done. You feel as though things will not get done, if you do not do them. Remember, you are no good for any one if you are not functioning properly. You have to be #1 to you.

The way to be #1 to you is to know about yourself. I have said this many times and I will continue to say it, *you have to know everything about yourself, to know your Character, to know who you really are.*

"HAVE SELF-ESTEEM"

I was in a relationship with a man for many years. I spent so much time learning about his Character, I neglected my own. I was so eager to please him. I knew his likes and dislikes. I felt that I could answer for him that is how well I felt that I knew him. Then several years and three children later we were no longer together and I had had absolutely no identity.

My mother did try to intervene. She knew the way that I was becoming was not in my Character. She would inquire about what was wrong with me all the time. She couldn't understand why I was having all these children out-of-wedlock and especially by this unfaith man. I had gone too far. I was desperately trying to please him. I wanted a two-parent home for my children. I wanted to make my 'family' work. I thought I needed to eventually become his wife. I did not realize that these insecurities that I possessed were cracks in my foundation.

My mother would tell me, "You do not have to have a baby every time he whispered he loves you, just say, "Uh huh, I love you, too" and go on about your business."

I thought that she just did not understand how much I "loved" this man. I did not grow up in a two-parent household and I was determined, at the time, my children would. Well, we all know the old saying, "why buy the cow, when you can get the milk for free?" Well, I was definitely giving away all of my milk for free. And each time he would hit or cheat on me, he was taking away pieces of my soul.

I was determined to "make" him love me. I was all he needed. I could be the woman he wanted. He didn't have to be with anyone else. I was bogged down with playing so many roles, trying to prove that I was a superwoman, I was ignoring the *'tick tock'* sounds ringing in my ears.

My problem was that I wanted to be loved so badly by him. My fulfillment was coming from his acceptance of me. I had this fairy tale image of how my life should be. It did not matter how much I would give, I may receive another baby, busted lip, or a black eye in return. Well, I was still determined to give even more. It must be something *I* was doing wrong. I definitely did not possess self-esteem. I was desperately looking for love and fulfillment through the acceptance of a man.

One day after an emotional argument, I sat on the edge of our bed crying, and he was about to leave out of the bedroom, he turned and looked at me and said "I made you into the woman that I wanted you to be" and he turned around and left. I sat there stunned. His words stung as if he had slapped my face. At that time, I did not fully realized that I did not know who I was, but the impact of his words, tugged at my soul for many years to come. I was so eager to pursue the knowledge of his Character, I wanted to know everything about him that I forgot about myself. In the meantime, he had been studying the *weaknesses* of my Character. He literally knew me better than I knew ME!

After many years had went by, I got use to the fact that this particular man was not for me, *but* I would move on to another man to fill that void. I was looking for my fulfillment through men. I had never given myself time to be alone, to heal my brokenness. I did not know how to separate being alone and being lonely. You can be alone, and not be lonely. I did not give myself time to get to know me. I never asked myself WHO AM I? If I had stopped and looked at my 'house'.... I had so many cracks, I was beginning to crumble.

I knew my exes' likes and dislikes, but I did not know my own. I knew their favorite color was blue and the other one's was black. What was my favorite color? Well, I didn't know, I guess I did not have one. I had lost my identity. I was the woman that they had molded me into, and not the woman that I needed to be. For all I knew, I could have been shaped into their mothers or their ex-girlfriends, or whomever. I did not know who I had become, but I did realize that I did not like what I was doing. I did not understand the depth of my Character. What am I really like? I needed to do a self-evaluation of my Character. *Who Am I Really?* I did not know. (We will discuss failed relationships more in my second book, *"Spending Years with the Wrong Man: How to get yourself together after a failed relationship"*).

"NO STANDING OVATIONS"

A lot of times women get in situations where they give more than they are receiving and it is because they are playing too many roles, the wrong roles. Make sure whatever role you are playing, it is the role that you have been assigned. Sometimes women can get so dramatic and take over the whole production. If we are not careful we can become like Eddie Murphy in the Nutty Professor movies. You will be one person playing all the roles. You are determined to play the whole cast, and you are only assigned to be the bellhop. So when your 'movie' flops, there is no one to blame but you.

I agree with Dr. Grace Cornish, author of *10 Good Choices that Empower Black Women's Lives,* on the fact that our lives are symbolic of a script. We all have roles to play and based on our life experiences, some scenes are better than others. But each "actor" has the ability to rewrite his or her own script. You have the power to determine how your production will end.

You have to know who you are, your Character, and the role that you have been assigned to play. You have to make sure that your Character is in alignment with your spirit and soul, and that you are content with your role. You will not have to try on all the costumes to play anyone else's roles. You will be able to give 100% to the role that you have been assigned.

Dr. Michele Owens-Patterson, a relationship therapist, says "no relationship is worth feeling bad about yourself. If being with your mate makes you feel inadequate and worthless, or makes you question whether you are good enough to be with him, then it is probably time for you to move on."

In my past failed relationships, I was being submissive to men who were not even my husbands, and in some cases, not even a devoted significant other. My Character had so many flaws, until I wasn't even a person. I was a puppet. I was so eagered to be attentive and please everyone else, but myself. I did not know what I wanted, needed, or who I was.... Character.... I was a girlfriend, lover, cook, his baby's mama, *his* mama, and anything else that he needed. I was all these things to a man, but a complete stranger to myself.

Relationship-wise, you are giving too much of yourself away too soon. I will reinforce again about women playing too many roles that they haven't been assigned to them. Stop being a 'wife', if you are only a girlfriend. Stop being his 'mother', if you are his wife. Stop being a 'dictator', if you are only a friend.

When you are giving all of yourself on Level 1, there will be nothing left of yourself to give on Level 10. So, if you have nothing left to offer.... You are not allowing yourself or the relationship time or room to grow. I have been guilty of this myself.

It should always go through a process and the process should be gradual. If you just jump out, wide open like, 'BAM! Here I am. Take it or leave it.' Do not be surprise if they decide to leave it. You are being too aggressive and if you are not careful, you may end up showing stalker tendencies.

So, when the relationship (of any kind) does ends, you are physically, mentally, maybe even financially, and most definitely emotionally wiped out. You are drained, depleted, and defeated. It could take years to get yourself nourished again. Other people would have moved on with their lives and you will be left hanging on to the "would'ves", "could'ves", and "should'ves". Stop trying to take on more than you can handle. You cannot nor should you have to perform all the roles. There are no standing ovations for being foolish.

"KEEP YOUR SANITY"

I was so in "love" with my ex that I was willing to do anything for him. He had many children before I met him, while I was with him, and after my relationship with him. He only had daughters, and I wanted to give him a son. So, after my first two daughters, I felt that the third time would be a charm, but I had another daughter. I ended up giving my baby up for adoption. I felt like a failure because I could not give him a son. That was my poor, misconstrued, unhealthy thoughts at the time. My child should have been my **first** priority, but she wasn't, it was him.

I had become sick and demented and was crying out for help. I needed to find myself and I needed to do it quickly. When your sanity and happiness depends upon whether or not someone else is happy, you will not make it. You are fighting a losing battle. You do not know how you are going to feel today until you see how the other person feels today. You do not know how your day is going to go until you see how their day is going. Your "downs" are their "ups". Your "ups" are their "downs.

It is like riding on an emotional roller coaster without any seatbelts on. It is dangerously unhealthy, and practically suicidal. When the wrong people know that they can control the strings to your heart, your feelings, your livelihood, your life, your Character…they can and will take advantage of you.

You are giving them too much power over you. Some people are not happy unless you are hurting. Have you ever been in a situation like that before? We train people how to treat us. You have to cut those strings. You are not a puppet. You are a person. Get your life back! It is your house. You can rebuild whenever you decide to. Learn to say No and learn to let go.

"SUPERWOMAN SYNODROME"

Keep moving forward. Do not look back. You cannot successfully move forward if you keep looking back. Begin to weed out the draining areas of your life. If you are not being replenished, you will be defeated, depleted, and ultimately deleted out.

Every trial and tribulation is an aide in the process of building your Character. The key is to know who you are and most importantly whose you are. You need compensations for your contributions. You need a full circle for balance. Everything must be a fair exchange, no bargaining. You have lent yourself out long enough. Sometimes you have to go 'borrow' yourself back. Let the people know that the 'lend' is over. Go and take yourself back! Go get you!

The Bible tells us that it is essential to be aware of wolves in sheep clothing. Everything that you perceive to be good *to* you may not be good *for* you. Everyone and everything is not suited for you. Your friend's Character does not have to be your Character. You have to be yourself. You have to make sure that the cycles of your life are balanced. Having balance is the key to your longevity. If the areas in your life are not adding up equally, then it is time for you to purge yourself of anyone or anything that is causing you discord.

You need to establish a relationship with the Lord. This relationship will give you the confidence that you need. You will not have the need to give away everything that you have/are in order to feel fulfilled. You will know that the very essence of your Character comes from self-fulfillment and not whatever leftovers or crumbs that someone thinks you should have.

So you are being so much to that person(s), you are so eager to please that person. You are proudly wearing that badge that reads, *"I AM A SUPERWOMAN!"* I can do everything you need; you do not have to look anywhere else. You are so quick to be a hero that you have totally neglected, rejected, and abandoned yourself. You are not a hero, that's being unrealistic. You are a human being with human limitations. You cannot be all things to all people at all times, and still have time to remain true to yourself. How can you give so much time, energy, and effort into loving and pleasing others and put yourself on the back burner?

Dr. Angela Neal-Barnett feels that some women need to take the *S* off their chest. Women refuse to admit that they are stressed and they keep their feelings bottled up inside while they help everyone else.

Dr. Neal-Barnett suggests that the next time a close friend asks you how you are doing and you are tempted to answer, "Fine," take a deep breath and then tell both of you the truth.

Ask yourself, how can I love someone for all the right reasons, when I do not love myself for any reason? When you are beating yourself up, being in a slump and depressed because you are overly pouring yourself into someone's life to get fulfillment. You can't be effective for anyone.

Another question I will like to pose to you. Are you giving so much to receive private or public glory? You need to assess the real reasons why you are giving. Are you giving so much of yourself to win friends or praise? Are you afraid to disappoint anyone? Are you clamoring for approval from people who do not even matter? Are you giving too much of yourself away?

"SETTING BOUNDARIES"

You have to give yourself time to research who you are. You have to know your Character so you will not be doomed to make the same mistakes. Do not deprive yourself. Your life is your own. You are too blessed to be stressed about anyone or anything. The very thing(s) that you are trying to hang on to could possibly be the very thing(s) you need to move away from. You need to declare your Independence.

Dr. Angela Neal-Barnett, says "extreme stress can increase your risk of heart disease, high blood pressure or stroke, and it can weaken your immune system." She believes that drama in your life could be the culprit.

Dr. Nancy H. Rosenberg, does not believe the solution to your stress has to be a one-time shot, a cure-all that will solve the problem with one easy notion. She believes that because pressure is coming at you from every direction, you'll need multiple angles to keep it at bay.

Dr. Rosenberg feels that you will need ways to keep your battery charged mentally, physically, and spiritually to help power through any crisis. She advises that, "you should; eat well, exercise, focus on the present, and rest."

Set your boundaries and demand others to respect them. If you do not respect your own standards, you can hardly expect anyone else to respect them. Do not be taken advantage of. Do not allow yourself to be taken for granted. Receive as much as you give. Give as much as you receive. Your Character requires a healthy cycle. A balance.

Do not deny yourself. You will crumble under the stress. Learn to say 'No', and not feel guilty about it. You cannot continue to overload yourself. Once again, you have to know who you are and whose you are. You are the daughter of a King. Baby, you are royalty, do not settle for less. Do not bargain or compromise your self-respect or integrity. Pray for wisdom. Know your self-worth and others will recognize it without you having to say a word.

HOW TO RECOGNIZE PEOPLE OR ACTIVITIES THAT YOU NEED TO 'WEED' OUT OF YOUR LIFE.

HONESTLY ANSWER THE FOLLOWING QUESTIONS.
* REPLACE WHATEVER NEEDS TO GO IN THE BLANK *

1. Does this <u>person</u> add to or take away from your life?

2. In what way is this <u>person</u> an asset or a liability?

3. How do you feel when this <u>person</u> is around?

4. How do you feel when this <u>person</u> is not around?

5. Does this <u>person</u> make you feel energetic, lively, or does this <u>person</u> zap your energy?

6. What are your contributions to this <u>person</u>?

7. Is there fair compensation for your contributions?

8. **Is there a fair exchange?**

9. **How would your life be different without this <u>person</u> in it?**

10. **How will you apply this assessment to your life?**

WHAT ARE YOUR THOUGHTS ABOUT CHAPTER 3?

WHAT HAVE YOU LEARNED FROM CHAPTER 3?

WHAT NECESSARY CHANGES CAN YOU MAKE TO YOUR CHARACTER FROM THE KNOWLEDGE THAT YOU GAINED FROM CHAPTER 3?

4

Battle Scars: Making It Through the Pain

"SCARS OR SCABS"

1. Have you ever gotten hurt as a child and it left a scar?

2. Can you remember the details of the incident?

3. Can you describe the exact pain of how bad it hurt? Or is it just a memory?

4. Do you consider your scars to be battle scars or avoidable accidents?

5. How do you avoid getting any scars now?

Chapter 4
Battle Scars: Making it through the Pain

"SURVIVING THE PAIN"

Some of our circumstances are so painful, that we would rather just ignore them rather than deal with them. You may ask yourself, 'if you decide to rebuild your Character, why couldn't you just start building on what you have today, instead of yesterday?'

Well, my sister, you are who you are today because of what happened to you on yesterday. I studied James Hutton in my Geology class. He said, "The key to the present is the past." This is so true. He was speaking about the solar system, but it also applies to the philosophy of our life, our Character.

We are who we are today because of our past experiences. You do not have to become a victim of your circumstances. You can overcome them and use them as a platform. A platform that is your center stage to display your strength. There is power in the old saying, "that whatever don't kill you will make you stronger". There is strength after the pain. You mature, gain wisdom, and power. You will survive the pain. You will know better the next time. You will not be so easy to crack under the pressure. You will not be so quick to whine that something hurts so badly.

God will be proud of you. He will say, "Okay, if you can handle *that*, I know that you will be able to handle *this*." The things that you suffer through privately, God will reward you for publicly. He will give you double for your trouble if you just go through the pain.

"YOU ARE WORTH IT!"

If you are going to war and fight for yourself, you may get all banged up. But you have to realize that you are worth fighting for. You have to tell yourself and believe what you say, "Whatever I have to go through for me, I am willing to do it. I am worth fighting for!" You have to be determined to make it. The pain is a necessary part of your process, but once you make it through, it will only be a memory.

The Holy Bible tells us in John 16:21 that, *a woman, when she is in labor, has sorrow because the hour has come; but as soon as she has given birth to the child, she no longer remembers the anguish, for joy that a human being has been born into the world.*

Any woman who has had a child knows the pain can be excruciating. The pain can become unbearable and indescribable. That same woman will tell you that when the baby is born and the pain is over, it is only a memory. That is why even though a woman knows how painful labor is; she still may continue to have more than one child. The labor was a pain that she had to go through to bring her baby forth, but once it was over, the pain was only a memory. Mothers consider it a labor of love. You need to love yourself enough to labor through your issues.

"SELF-DISCOVERY"

When you begin to research what traits make up your Character, you have to be ready to discover everything about yourself. You have to be willing to sort through the good, the bad, and the ugly. Some discoveries will be messier than others. When you decide to rebuild your foundation, you have to be open to what you may find. You have to go in with a positive attitude and not be discouraged.

You need to put on your hard hat, goggles, and begin drilling until you hit bottom. You have to be prepared to stay there no matter what you find out about yourself. If you choose to run away without doing the necessary repairs, you will never find out who you really are. You might not like what you find, but that is why you are rebuilding, to correct any problems.

This is no time to feel sorry for yourself. You do not need to throw a pity party, because no one is coming. Once you have your house finish, you can throw a coming out party or a house warming party. Then it is time to celebrate and even then if no one comes, you still throw yourself a party. You can celebrate the 'real you' coming out. You deserve it!

"DO NOT QUIT"

Rebuilding is essential to becoming renewed and having longevity. You do not want to worry about any cracks showing up when you least expect them or just completely collapsing under the pressure. You have to be ready to go through the pain. This is not going to be a walk in the park. I have learned that when you go through a lot, you will also suffer a lot. If you are 20 years old, then you have 20 years worth to sort out. It has taken years for you to be molded into the person you are today. There will be a process that you will have to endure in order to shed the old you and become transformed into the new you.

Your Character has issues that need to be sorted out. You have to deal with them and it will not happen overnight. If you just begin the process, be patient, remain consistent; it will happen.

The pain is not there to cripple you. It is there to enable you. By dealing with the pain of your past helps you to strive even harder to reach for a brighter future. It will get better.

Surviving the pain will give you a sharper eye, alert ears, a strong sense of smell, and a keen taste to know when there is danger. Experiencing pain gives you an alertness about yourself to sense an unwelcome invasion of your being. You gain a great sense of intuition and judgment when something is not in alignment with your spirit and soul. You will be able to recognize that what looks good, may not be good for you. It may seem okay, but you will know if it is not in alignment with you and you will not be willing to jeopardize your Character by associating with it.

"OPENING AND CLOSING YOUR DOORS"

No one has control over your life but you. No one should be able to come into your life unless they are invited. When you are on the outside in the world, you can handle the outside world accordingly. When you arrive at your home, your safe haven, and shut your door…the world and the drama that comes with it is on the other side of that door. No one or nothing on the outside can enter into the inside, unless you open your door and invite them in. Your 'home' is your temple. You must it accordingly.

You have control over that door, your doorknob, and your choices. You have control over your life. When we open certain doors in our lives, we must face the consequences of our decisions. Some of these consequences are painful, because of the choices that we have made. It is possible to have some doors opened that you need to close. If your choices are not compatible to whom you are or whom you are trying to become, it may be time to close those doors.

You cannot continue to ignore the pain and expect to become a better person. You must face the pain and heal in order to become a better person. If you do not allow yourself to properly heal, you are leaving wounds exposed. They are susceptible to infections. You are allowing an entryway for infectious bacteria to come in and contaminate your Character.

"TURNING A NEGATIVE INTO A POSITIVE"

Allow yourself to self-heal. Allow yourself the appropriate amount of time to go through your Character's metamorphosis. Allow the hurt worm to go inside its cocoon to redevelop, recondition, rechannel, and redirect all of its energy. You have to eliminate all the negativities. When the process is done, you will be able to gain the strength you need to emerge as a confident, strong, positive, and beautiful butterfly. Now, it is important to allow the proper time for the procedure to take place. Coming out too soon can lead to underdevelopment and/or setbacks.

You cannot give up. You have to continue to work hard and know that your power is on the other side of the pain. It may seem like it is a long and scary dark path to travel, but you must pray to the Lord for help. He will light your way with a pillar of fire.

Have you ever paid attention to a bad thunderstorm? I mean it is really raining so hard and heavy, it is almost scary. It gets so dark outside. The wind is high, the lightening is flashing, and the thunder is roaring. The rain is so heavy. It seems to be coming down in sheets, strong enough to wash away anything in its path. This description sounds pretty bad, doesn't it? Well, this thunderstorm is symbolic of your life and it's pain.

You think this is horrible. You feel like, it's too bad, that you cannot go through it. You may feel like you cannot face the pain. It is too powerful. You cannot see anything good coming from your suffering. What could possibly be beneficial coming out of this thunderstorm? What positive can come from this negative?

Now, have you ever witnessed the end results of a thunderstorm? The sun comes out shining more brightly than before the thunderstorm. The sky is so blue. Its heavenly. The clouds look so white and fluffy looking, you can hear the birds chirping and sometimes even a beautiful rainbow will appear. You wonder how something so beautiful can come out of something that seemed so bad. This is symbolic of your life and its pain.

After you go through your storm(s), face your pain and get rid of all your negatives, so that all your positives can be seen. You have to allow the pain to surface, so you can be fully cleansed and purified. You do not want any traces of left over residue traces left in your spirit. You want the beautiful colors of your rainbow to be reflected inwardly and outwardly through your Character.

Some of your best lessons come from trial and error. You do not know what is going to work for you until you try it. Again, I will say most of our pain comes from the choices we have made in our lives. Some of the pain stems from the decisions made during our childhood, either by us or someone else.

As children, we are very innocent and easy to be influence as well being easy to be manipulated. We are trusting and believe that we are going to be okay. We should be protected. This is how it supposes to be. But sometimes we have to learn the hard way that this is not always the case. Our guardians, other adults, or just people in general have made decisions concerning us, either about us or to us, that has left an impact on our lives.

"GOD IS FOR YOU"

It is not too late to break free of the past. Yes, the past makes you who you are today, but it is not suppose to consume your whole being. A lot of things that you have gone through may not have been your fault. You have to recognized that and know that you do not need to feel guilty, dirty, or ashamed of anything that has happened to you that you had no control over. You do not have to feel that way if you did have control during that time. What happened to you does not define who you are. You are able to overcome anything. Do not allow what people have said or have done break your spirit.

One of my favorite scriptures in the Holy Bible is Psalm 27. It reads, *"The Lord is my light and my salvation; Whom shall I fear? The Lord is the strength of my life; Of whom shall I be afraid? When the wicked came against me, To eat up my flesh, My enemies and foes, They stumbled and fell. Though an army encamp against me, My heart shall not fear; Though war may rise against me, In this I will be confident.... Wait on the Lord; Be of good courage, And He shall strengthen your heart; Wait, I say, on the Lord!"*

This scripture is so powerful. It is universal for what ever you may be or have been going through. You do not have to worry about others, just know that the Lord will do whatever you ask of Him. I read a saying that read, "Jesus paid a debt that he did not owe because we had a debt that we could not pay." Isn't that wonderful. Whatever we have done or whatever has been done to us, we can overcome it. We just need to rebuild. Others may have placed baggage on you, but the pain is still something *you* have to deal with.

"NO SUBSTITUTES"

You cannot include people when dealing with your issues. So many of us would like to hide behind someone else instead of facing our issues head on. Let us get something straight now; you can't substitute pain with people! It will not work. When you are hurt, you do not make good decisions. When you are hurt, you can possibly hurt others.

When you are hurting, you cannot make clear and rash decisions. You are not able think as clearly or function as properly. You do not need people, food, drugs, or alcohol when you are facing your pain. You do not need to feel numb. You need to feel the raw pain to be able to fully appreciate the benefits from it.

Yes, there are benefits. You have to let the old you literally die. You have to allow yourself time to grieve. During this grieving process, you have to be willing to forgive yourself and others for their trespasses against you. Arise and go forth before the Lord and let Him breathe new life into you. Then you need to be ready to welcome the new you, the 'real you', your new Character into existence.

You need to be able to expose you to you. Issues that you have suppressed and allowed to lay dormant, needs to be revealed. This is the only way to be truly healed. This allows the true aspects of who you are to surface and be released.

The very thing that can make you whole lies within you. I often wondered about women who go to bed with makeup on. It is the end of the day. The outside world is on the other side of the door. They should feel safe and secure in their own homes. So why do they feel the need to prep up and get in full costume before they go to sleep?

Some wives will not even let their husbands see them without their makeup on. Why not? Their Character is suffering tremendously because they have to be fake all the time. They do not have an outlet for their true identity. They cannot be real, even when they are sleeping. They have not been able to relax, or gotten rest or had a peace of mind because they are literally behind a mask twenty-four hours a day.

When we do not allow our real selves to emerge, we are behind a mask 24/7. That is no way to live. You are not being fair to your loved ones and most importantly, you are not being true to yourself. When you cannot be the 'real you' at all times, you are practically living in a prison within yourself.

It is time to confront any hidden issues and face the pain. I am not saying that life has to always be so hard. But when it is, do not try to run away from it. Deal with it. It is time to go to your foundation and work your way up to discover who you really are. Your life is your own. You should be able to truly enjoy it by being the 'real you' at all times.

Realizing that you cannot substitute pain with people or other excuses will make you have to stand on your own two feet. Sometimes you have to go through whatever you have to go through, and sometimes that means facing it alone. You have to go through your metamorphosis process. *You have to go through your Struggle-in your Situation-to gain Strength-for your Success.*

Some things are your necessities. You have to go through them. You have to go through tests to have a testimony. You have to go through pain to become powerful, to make progress. You have to go through struggles to become a survivor. So many of you do not want to allow the pain to help build your Character. Your plight can help someone else. You have to let this process help define your Character.

Romans 5:3-5 tell us, *that we should glory in the tribulations, knowing that tribulation produces perseverance. And perseverance, character; and character, hope. New hope does not appoint, because the love of God has been poured out in our hearts by the Holy Spirit who was given to us.*

"BELIEVE IN YOURSELF"

You have to have the diligence to make it through. You have to allow yourself to let the pain shape, mold, and develop you into a stronger person. Do not pull someone into your life, you must let your foundation completely dry. You are almost complete. Do not stop short of your completion, by looking for a hero.

Do not believe that you need a person to complete you, fulfill you, save you, or to fill that void that is in your life. Stop being needy. You have to possess your own power. You cannot rely on 'quick fixes' to get through your pain. You do have to go through something in order to get something. Life is all about choices. Do not feel that you will never be able to recover from any decisions that you have made in your past. Tomorrow is always a new day to make new decisions. You can always reinvent yourself. You have the opportunity to do better. I feel that life follows a pattern. This may apply to some and not to others. Some people do mature faster than others, but it is never too late to mold your Character in a decent, moral being.

I believe in this Life Philosophy;

20s—finding yourself
30s—correcting what you have done in your 20s
40s—getting stability
50s & up—being stable, comfortable, loving life and the skin you are in

You need a Character that is whole. When confronted with the question *Who Am I?* You should not have to wait for someone else to answer for/about you. You should be fulfilled and not lacking in any area. You have to face the pain and conquer it. Let it become just a memory. Be proud of the 'real you' because you have made it through. God wants to give you a break through. He got to break you, so that you will be through! You will survive the pain.

HONESTLY ANSWERS THESE QUESTIONS:

"ARE YOU HEALING?"

1. What visible or invisible scars do you have on you right now?

2. Are these scars physical, emotional, mental, verbal, financial, or all the above?

3. Have you given yourself time to properly heal?

4. How have you handled the pain of your scars?

5. Are you easily scarred?

6. Why or why not?

7. Are you still battling? With yourself or someone else?

8. Why or why not?

WHAT ARE YOUR THOUGHT ABOUT CHAPTER 4?

WHAT HAVE YOU LEARNED FROM CHAPTER 4?

WHAT ARE THE NECESSARY CHANGES THAT YOU CAN MAKE IN YOUR CHARACTER FROM THE KNOWLEDGE THAT YOU HAVE GAINED FROM CHAPTER 4?

5

Foundation: Building on Solid Ground

"Starting at ground level and working your way up."

The Webster Dictionary defines foundation as *the act of founding or establishing; the basis on which anything is founded. An institution supported by an endowment; a cosmetic base for make-up.*

The Holy Bible tells us in Luke 6:47-49 that, *"Whoever comes to Me 'Lord, Lord,' and not do the things which I say? He is like a man building a house, who dug deep and laid the foundation on the rock. And when the flood arose, the stream beat vehemently against that house, and could not shake it, for it was founded on the rock." But he who heard and did nothing is like a man who built a house on the earth without a foundation, against which the stream beat vehemently; and immediately it fell. And the ruin of that house was great."*

Your Character is your "home". But in order, to have a safe, happy, productive, and strong "home", you must have a strong foundation. What is your home built upon? Is it concrete or sinking sand?

Coming into the realization of what you are built upon is the first step. Now, if you are built on a faulty, shifty slab are you willing to rebuild? That is the million-dollar question. You have to be willing to go back in and correct, possibly years of, unsatisfactory work.

The procedure can be painful, long, and hard, but the end-result will be the ultimate satisfaction and completion. You will have an impeccable Character/ "house" built on a qualified, strong, and stable foundation. Get ready to be built on solid ground, baby! Get your tools and let's go to work!......

"STARTING AT GROUND ZERO"

Foundation is very important. It is the basis of our Character. It is the pinnacle of who we really are. Everything we have been through, anyone we have encountered in our life, has contributed to our foundation. Our foundation is the platform, the center stage the core to our souls, to our Character.

You have your foundation, then the many levels that make up your 'house'. Your house is symbolic of *you*. Your foundation is ground zero. It is necessary to have the most reliable tools to lay a sturdy, stable, reliable foundation. All the levels of your Character is built upon this foundation. Your foundation has to be secure enough to handle these levels if not, your foundation could completely collapse under the weight of your life.

"HAVE THE RIGHT BLUEPRINTS AND TOOLS"

To begin to build your foundation, you have to decide who you are and who you want to become. You need blueprints. You have to decide whether you are going with blueprints of Person A or Person B. Most importantly, please allow God be the architecture of your plans. Now, you must have the proper tools for either person. The tools are a necessity. The good thing is, you already possess the necessary tools within you to build.

You may want to build a house, but the only tool that you have is a screwdriver. Now, that screwdriver is definitely not going to build a whole house, no matter what size the house will be. The screwdriver can help, but there is no way that it will be the only tool that you will need. Tools are very important, but the proper tools are essential.

Now, let's inspect Person A and Person B's blueprints. You need to decide which plan you will model your 'home' after. Person A's levels consist of: God, integrity, love, intelligence, humbleness, respect, confidence, politeness, and forgiveness. Person B's levels consist of: loneliness, anger, withdrawal, spite, bitterness, selfishness, backbiting, hatred, and unforgiveness.

"INSPECTION"

Now, decide which person you are and which person you would like to become. In order to become whichever person you want to become, no matter which person that you may be right now (because you can change), you have to prepare to get your foundation ready to be built on. Your foundation is what makes you…you.

It is important to inspect your foundation for cracks and flaws. If you build on a faulty foundation, it will not work. The appearance may look good on the outside, but as the years go by everything will begin to shift. Your cracks will begin to show. Before long, cracks will be running up the walls in plain view for everyone to see.

Your cracks will become exposed. Little secrets will begin to seep out. So do not put in years of building a huge, wonderful, spectacular 'house' for the public to admire. Do not be in such a hurry to impress people for 'show off' purposes, and build on a faulty foundation.

If your foundation isn't solid and stable, the exterior/interior of your house will not be stable. So do not waste your time building a quick castle only for it to collapse when the first turbulence comes against it. Take the required time to get your foundation right, so your 'house' will be right. The process may become painful, but as I said before, the end result will be worth it.

The most important fact to remember while building a solid foundation for your new home is to invest in the full coverage, dependable, trustworthy home insurance of God. With the Lord's insurance on your house, your home will become a secure, safe haven and it will be able to handle any adversity that may come against it. No cracks are allowed here. Get yourself together, so that your 'house' may be in order.

"SPEAKING POWER INTO YOUR FOUNDATION"

FOUNDATION! You have to build on what you believe. You have to instill into yourself that you are worthy. Say out loud; "I am worthy", "I am wonderful", "I am deserving", "I am powerful", "I am important", "I am lovable", "I am truth", "I am Me!"

You have to instill these beliefs into your foundation. The Bible tells us that "as a man thinketh, so is he". You have to speak encouraging words to yourself on a daily basis, until they come to pass. Claim what you want for your life. *Everything* is possible.

Everyone is valuable. Each and every person has a divine purpose for his or her life. You need to pray to God to reveal your purpose. God gives us signs all the time. He can be as subtle as a gentle tap on the shoulder or as blunt as running into a brick wall, either way He *will* gain our attention. So, in case we have missed some clues, we must retrace our steps. Ask yourself the following questions, and answer them honestly.

Where are you at in your life at this very moment?

How did you arrive at this point?

Did you turn left when you should have turned right?

Are you on the right path now?

Do you need to make a U-turn?

Did you learn from your experiences?

Answer these questions with the first thoughts that come into your mind. Assess your answers, on a separate sheet if necessary. Evaluate your honest answers. Are your answers something that you have always known or did you surprise yourself? When you implore your thoughts, also explore your true feelings and emotions. *Implore* to *Explore* and become *Exposed* to yourself.

"GETTING TO THE ROOT"

It is very important to make the experience a lesson, and gain helpful knowledge about yourself from it. Do not just be experienced, like a guinea pig, but learn from your experiences. You can take something from every single thing that has ever happened to you in your life. Consider your mistakes as opportunities to learn something about yourself.

Your foundation is the most crucial part of your development. It is the ROOT. So when you go to reassess your life, you cannot start at the top and go down. You simply cannot do that. You must start at the bottom, the root, and work your way up! Therefore when your root is firmly planted, the development of the fruits of your Character can begin to grow. You will be able to produce what you've been planted in.

The Holy Bible tells us in Luke 8: 5-18 that, *"A sower went out to sow his seed. And as he sowed, some fell by the wayside; and it was trampled down, and the birds of the air devoured it. Some fell on rock; and as soon as it sprang up, it withered away because it lacked moisture. And some fell among thorns, and the thorns sprang up with it and choked it. But others fell on good ground, sprang up, and yielded a crop a hundredfold."* When He had said these things He cried, *"He who has ears to hear, let him hear!" "To you it has been given to know the mysteries of the kingdom of God, but to the rest it is given in parables, that 'Seeing they may not see, And hearing they may not understand.'" "Now the parable is this: The seed is the word of God. Those by the wayside are the ones who hear; then the devil comes and takes away the word out of their hearts, lest they should believe and be saved. But the ones on the rock are those who, when they hear, receive the word with joy; and these have no root, who believe for a while and in time of temptation fall away. Now the ones that fell among thorns are those who, when they have heard, go out and are choked with cares, riches, and pleasures of life, and bring no fruit to maturity. But the ones that fell on good ground are those who, having heard the word with a noble and good heart, keep it and bear fruit with patience. No one, when he has lit a lamp, covers it with a vessel or puts it under a bed, but sets it on a lampstand, that those who enter may see the light. Therefore take heed how you hear. For whoever has, to him more will be given; and whoever does not have, even what he seems to have will be taken from him."*

So, you have to make sure your foundation, your root, is right because if not, when you produce, it will be exposed. You will definitely reap what you sow. I read a saying on a poster, "we can not change unless we survive, but we can not survive unless we change." That is so true. We have to learn to adapt, and by doing that sometimes we pick up things from our environment, whether it is positive or negative.

It would be unrealistic not to believe that our encounter with people and our environment does not make on impact on our Character. It is safe to say that our daily interactions leave their own significant traces upon our persona.

The key is to begin at the foundation, your childhood. So many things that we have gone through in our childhood plays an important role in molding us into adults. We can harbor great insecurities or allude confidence from elements of our childhood.

Our reactions, emotions, manners, and self-esteem all stems from what has been deposited, voluntarily or involuntarily, into our foundation. So, we must begin an intense search of our inner beings. I already said that you literally have to turn yourself inside out. You have to probe your very essence, your spirit. What characterizes you is located within your spirit. It is the origin of where you begin and end.

Your intuition your radar that lives within your spirit. Have you ever said or heard someone else say, "That just did not feel right?" or "I wanted to do it, but it just didn't feel right in my spirit?'

Sometimes when you are not thinking clearly, you have to go inside and trust your gut instincts. When you have cloudy judgments, things may appear to be in a daze. Jon Gordon, M.A., author of *"Become an Energy Addict: Simple, Powerful Ways to Energize Your Life"*, says that "your inner spirit is connected to a brighter reality." He feels that our inner voice is a source of wisdom that will lead us into the direction in which we should go. He believes that in our time of doubt that we should allow that higher source of power to guide us back to clarity/reality.

Something that has been already deposited in your foundation, it has been imparted onto your spirit. It lets you know when something is right or wrong. You may not be able to put your finger on it right now, but "something"/intuition/spirit tells you it isn't right.

The next element that is embedded into your foundation is your soul. Your soul is defined as *the spirit in mind that is believed to be separate from the body and is the source of a person's emotional, spiritual and moral nature.*

Your soul gives you; your emotions, morals, and layers of spiritual attributes wrapped up into the physical. Your sensitiveness, hardness, securities or insecurities can derive from your soul. Your soul gives you your depth as a person. How deep are you? Are you a deep or shallow person? How intense are you? How much can you comprehend?

Depth is so important when you are searching and rebuilding your foundation because there may be some uglies that have gotten hidden. When you decide to go back and tamper with your foundation, some hidden secrets may fall out of some hidden places. So, you have to be strong and stable enough to search through the good stuff and the messes.

The reward is, the deeper you go in your mess and clean it up, the higher up you can go and be glorified in the Lord. No more hidden messes, no more shames, no more doubts, no more insecurities, and no more mountains in your way. The Bible tells us if we have the faith of a mustard seed we can do remarkable things. We can speak to a mountain and tell it to move and it will *have* to move. So, whatever your mountains are they can be moved. Isn't it awesome to possess that type of power within us?

We have stored a lot of *mountains* in us from our childhood that we never had moved. We just learned to live with them and go around them. Eventually you will realize that with all that maneuvering you will become exhausted. You cannot see around a mountain and there is no telling what could be on the other side. Let's just clear our path of the mountains and be able to travel freely.

"EVERYONE HAS A PAST"

Everyone has a past. You would not be human if you did not have one. We all have been in situations. Some situations were because of our decisions and some situations are the results of other people's decisions. When going into your foundation and dealing with past issues, you do have to distinguish whether some actions that has taken place in your life were the results of your own intentions or someone else's choices. You should not carry the blame or guilt for situations that you did not have any control over.

Whatever the case may be, it is never too late to live your life with morals and self-respect. You can always step back and re-evaluate yourself and make the necessary changes to improve your Character. You are in control of your life. You have the authority and the ability to regulate and direct your life. I want to put an emphasis on *You*.

In my early teens, I always wanted to hang around this particular group of girls. The family had just moved to my neighborhood from a large city. The family consisted of a single mother and four daughters. They all seemed like a tight-knit family. The mother allowed the daughters to use profanity and have their boyfriends spend the night at their house. The daughters were able to do practically whatever they desired to do.

Well, of course at the time, this seemed very appealing to a teenager. I thought this family was great and so did a lot of other teenagers that hung out at their home. They would always have parties with large crowds any day of the week. There was always something happening at their house.

One night after a party, I was walking home with a guy, who was my neighbor and supposedly my friend. We laughed and joked along the way and as we got near my home, he snatched me by the arm and pulled me inside a vacant house. He raped me. I fought him at first, and then it just became unreal to me.

It was like a moment of, *"this can't be happening to me"*. I just laid there. He got off of me when he finished and had pulled his pants up while I was still just lying there on the floor. He extended his hand to help me up and I took it and stood. He took a couple steps across the room to get my pants and panties and it was at that moment that I realized that I was naked from the waist down. It all seemed to have happened so fast.

I hurriedly put my panties on and then my pants and as I looked around for my flip-flop sandals on, he said, "Your pants are inside out." I just mumbled that it was okay. I had found my sandals by then and had run out of the house to my home.

I was shaking so bad. I ran into my bathroom and threw up. I put my clothes in a paper sack and threw them away. I filled the bathtub with very hot water. While the bath water was running, I sat on the edge of the tub, looking at myself in a full-length mirror mounted on the back of our bathroom door, crying and shaking, I asked myself "What just happened?" When I sat in the tub, the water was so hot, it turned my skin red, but really it was not hot enough. I sat in the tub for hours, until the water turned cold. I just sat there too numb to move.

It was about two weeks later; I was back at the 'party' house again. I told the girls what had happened to me. They in return told a few more girls who came over what had happened to me. Then it became a question and answer session, but more like an interrogation session. I did not want to feel all weird or be cast out. So, I immediately regretted revealing what had happened to me, so I recanted my story. I went from being 'raped' to just 'doing it' with him. Now, that was acceptable to the group.

I mean he was a guy from the neighborhood who hung out with us, so of course he was not really a bad guy...So, if he just had 'sex' with me, it would be handled a lot better than the truth. I just figured the lie would be better. I had already been humiliated privately; I did not think I could handle being humiliated publicly, too. I chalked it up to 'knowing exactly what I was doing.' I did not realized that selling myself out, would cost me so much later in my adult life.

After that moment, I put it behind me. I had suppressed what had happened to me in the very deep, dark corners of my mind. I continued to hang out with them. I continued to hang out with him. As far as what had happened, it didn't happened. I actually had suppressed my rape so deep, I did not think of it again, until about two years ago. I had begun researching my foundation. I had begun to do a self-evaluation on my Character, and this was one of those hidden messes that were in a hidden place in my foundation.

My house was beautiful on the outside, but some cracks were beginning to show. I could not investigate the walls, where the cracks were showing, I had to go to my foundation and work my way up. I had to get to the source, the beginning, of my cracks. My rape, that I so long thought that I had put behind me and never properly dealt with, was a major crack.

"YOUR CRACKS WILL SHOW UP"

Now, I am just going to tell you, when you begin to rebuild, it can get ugly. You will have to face all the things that you had placed in those secrets corners. You will have to deal with those little spots where the cement is still wet. You did not even let dry, before you begin to build. You are going to have to go in and take out the cheap materials where you tried to cut cost, because it is true, you do get what you pay for.

When my rape's crack began to surface, I was truly floored. I had to allow myself to go through a lot of raw feelings and emotions that I did not allow myself to previously go through. I had begun the process that night of the incident, but I never got to continue through it. I chose to block it out instead of going through a healing process. Every healing process deals with pain. I did not allow myself to fully go through the pain, so I was never fully healed. I never dealt with my invasion, so therefore it had no way to exit, it just got stored into my foundation. Unbeknownst to me, it was secretly one of the traits of my Character.

Once my rape became re-known to me again, I couldn't ignore it. I had to face it, because it would not be so easily forgotten this time. Nor, did I want to forget it. I needed to discover my true Character. I asked myself, *"Who am I really?"* I knew my genetic make-up. My parents were the cause of that. I needed to know my characteristic make-up. I am basically the cause of that.

So, I prayed. I asked the Lord, to help me find out true identity. I needed to know what defines *Keke*. I know where I am right now, but I needed to assess where I came from, to have a sense of where I am going. I needed to go within myself to find myself. Wouldn't it be terrible to live your whole life and not know your true Character, your true identity? In Genesis 32: 27-28, God asked Jacob what was his name. Jacob had lived his whole life as one person, but he was actually someone else. His whole identity had changed. It had changed for the better.

Now, if someone to ask you who you are it would seem silly for you to hesitate to answer, because of course you should know your name. But what if you went your whole life believing that you were one person, but you were actually someone else. What if you believe you were a "Jacob" but you were actually "Israel"?

When you find out who you are, you do not have to keep looking back. You need this knowledge to move forward. You really have to handle whatever needs to be handled and tie up loose ends. Please, equip yourself with the necessary tools to go in and rebuild your foundation. I prayed for the will to do this and for the ability to see what lays dormant. You have to pray for the knowledge and the strength to make the necessary repairs to your Character. Armed with these words and the Lord's tools, baby put on your hardhat, goggles, and get your drill ready and go to work! If anyone steps on your broken pieces and inquire about what is going on, just put out a sign that reads, "Under Construction!" and keep on drilling.

My rape was a crack, being a single mother was a crack, being passive and submissive was a crack, being withdrawn was also a crack. I ran into some cracks that were worst than others and I found some that were very small and just beginning. As I was stepping around my foundation, it was a little shaky. I knew while I was repairing, I needed to fix everything. I had an issue with men. I really wanted a two-parent household. I was having the children, but didn't have a husband. I was going through so much with a man, but getting so little in return.

I had to face my crack of unfulfillment. I was looking for my self-love, stability, and security through someone else. I had to deal with my Character's neediness. All these cracks began at my foundation. Whatever your cracks are, you have to be prepared to go within your foundation and work your way up, because when you build on a solid and stable foundation, you build yourself into a strong and stable person with great Character.

HONESTLY ANSWER THE FOLLOWING QUESTIONS:

1. What kind of Foundation do you have?

2. Is it more like concrete or sinking sand?

3. What issues in your Foundation are beginning to show cracks?

4. Do you realize a solid and stable Foundation leads to strong Character?

5. Are you willing to rebuild your Foundation?

6. Are you ready to face some cracks that have or will surface?

7. Do you know that you can do ALL things through Christ, whom strengthens you?

Get ready to be the 'real you' at all times. Get Rest, Have Peace, Love Yourself, and Enjoy Life.

WHAT HAVE YOU LEARNED FROM CHAPTER 5?

WHAT ARE YOUR THOUGHTS ABOUT CHAPTER 5?

WHAT STEPS CAN YOU TAKE TO MAKE THE NECESSARY CHANGES IN YOUR CHARACTER FROM THE KNOWLEDGE YOU GAINED FROM CHAPTER 5?

6

Finally! Becoming the 'Real' Me

"EVOLVING"

Alright! You are finally at the end of your metamorphosis process. Finally, you are 'becoming' the 'real you'. The key word is *becoming*. Learning who you really are is always a process. But now you do have a strong indication of who you definitely are not. You can precisely pinpoint specifics about your Character. You are able to sense what does or does not align up with your spirit.

Let's review what we have learned thus far. We have learned about; knowing the aspects of your Character; rebuilding your foundation; prioritizing the 4 departments of your Character; we determined whether you are giving more than you are receiving; and we have established that you have to go through the pain during your transformation. Great, now you are on the right on track. You are ready to go onto the next phase and move forward.

You cannot move forward, if you are constantly looking back. You cannot continue to live in the past. You must revisit your past in order to learn from it, but you do not need to stay there. You have to realize that your past is just that, your past. It is over and done with. You cannot change what has happened, but you can change you. You have to know that your past does not have to define who you are today. You can be renewed, with the renewing of your mind and your heart. You have to have forgiveness in your life.

"LEARN TO FORGIVE"

You are bigger than whatever you have done or been through. There are issues in your life that you need to forgive others for. There are situations in your life that you need to forgive yourself for. You cannot continue to carry around the heavy burden of guilt weighing you down for the rest of your life. You need to loose that bondage and set yourself free.

Jon Gordon, an energy coach and author of *"Energy Addict: 101 Mental, Physical, & Spiritual Ways to Energize Your Life"*, suggests that if you have been hurt or betrayed, you do not have to hold on to that negative energy. Gordon believes that letting go makes space for the positives, such as peace, joy, and love to enter your life. According to Gordon, you're doing it more than just for the person that you are forgiving. You are doing it for yourself.

"THE PAST IS OVER"

You cannot be like Lot's wife in Genesis 19:26, and continue to look back, because it will destroy you. Once you have finally decided to become who you really are. You have to let go of the past. Yesterday is essential to help you build but you can't live in the past. Today is here and tomorrow is fresh and waiting for you. When you get your Character right, you will truly walk into your destiny and what God has for you.

"PLANT GREAT SEEDS"

You have to always remember; the rebuilding begins with your foundation. Foundation is so important. It is the key in making you, you. It begins with your childhood. Your life is your ground, your soil. You allow whatever seeds to be planted there. You have control over what seeds germinate in your soil. If you water those seeds or if you even entertain them, they will grow. They can help you or they can hinder you. This all plays a part in your Character's make up.

The Bible tells us in John 15:1-27, in summary, *If you are productive, your branches will bear fruit, but if not your branches will wither away. Be useful, so you may reap the productive fruits.* Your being is wonderful because God chose you. You are chosen. Now, you must do your part. You have to determine, what the fruits of your labor will be.

You have to make up your mind to only think positive thoughts. Nothing should ever be so bad, that it just throws you completely off track. Now, I am not talking about tragedies. Just do not allow yourself to be victimize and remain a victim. If you remain a victim, then you are truly losing out.

"GET INTO 'THE KNOW'"

If you begin to look at every situation and take the negative out, there is a positive. Know your self-worth. Know your values. Know your strengths and weaknesses. Know your talents. Know your passions. Know your goals. Know your purpose. Know the Truth. Know You! You know how you hear your favorite song, and you instantly know that it is your favorite song, by the music before you even hear a word? Well, you should have that same type of instant familiarity with yourself. Know you!

So, finally becoming the 'real you' means to get reacquainted with yourself. You have to think positive about yourself. Every thought about yourself should be positive. The Bible tells us; *as a man thinketh, so is he/she*. If you think you are nothing, that is the results you will reap for yourself…NOTHING!

"NO MORE DRAMA"

When you are positive and feel good about yourself, the sky is the limit. You have no drama in your Character, so therefore you want no drama in your life. This is a part of your process in finally becoming the 'real you'. You have to renew your mind and pray for an understanding of the different areas in your life. You have to think and be positive. You also have to renew your heart. Address the issues that are in your heart, face them and let them go. Do not harbor any iniquities in your heart. *Address, Face, and Release.*

Now your mind is clear, your heart is new, and your spirit and soul is cleansed. Claim what you want for your life. Claim what you want in your life. When you get a new outfit, shoes, or get your hair or make up professionally done, it makes you feel brand new. When you have a makeover, it makes you look good on the outside and gives you an uplift on the inside. As long as your makeover lasts, you feel great; your attitude is great.

Well, that is how it feels when your Character gets a makeover. When you are being the 'real you' at all times, you feel great everyday. You can always have a positive attitude. You will look wonderful on the outside and feel great on the inside.

"LIVE YOUR LEGACY"

You have to live your life today, the way you wish to be remembered forever. Your name is very important. A person automatically knows something about you, whether it is good or bad, when they hear your name. Your Character is the epitome of your integrity, honesty, creditability, and dependability. Proverbs 22:1-29 tells about the value of a good name. Verse 1 says, *"A good name is to be chosen rather than great riches."*

When your morals are in perspective, so is your word. Your reputation precedes you. You want your Character to have depth, to stand for something. I use to wonder why a lot of award shows were posthumously honoring people. Allow yourself to be celebrated today, even if you are the only one celebrating.

You should treat others, the way yourself wish to be treated and respected. Respect, grace, and humanity should be traits of your Character. If you are a hell raiser, people will remember that. A conversation about you could go like this:

Person A: "Girl, you know Ms. So and So died?"
Person B: "Yeah, you remember she was so bitchy and mean?"
Person A: "You can say that again. She is probably in hell, giving the devil trouble right now!"

If we think about great figures in our history and even presently, these people lived and is living their legacy. So when they had passed away, that's how they were able to leave a legacy behind. You can't falsify a legacy for someone. They must already possess it. Remember, choose to live each day, the way you wish to be engraved forever. Do not let your living be in vain. You must find out your purpose. Do not put your Character into question. Please do not jeopardize your Character.

Your Character is a daily representation of you. You can imitate what you think others want to see, but you can only perpetrate for so long. When the 'real you' begins to show through the cracks, what do you do then? If you have to be fake all the time and put on a false show every time that you go out, then you are being completely worthless. You have lost your own sense of worth. Matthews 5:13-16 tells us *"that you are the salt of the earth, but if you lose your flavor, how shall you be seasoned? You become good for nothing and may as well be trampled underfoot by men."* The feet of the same men and women that you are trying to impress.

"BE CONFIDENT"

You are the light within your own life. You need to be pivotal. *You* need to matter to *you*. You should be able to shine so brightly that when you walk into a room, people will be able to look at you and see your good heart, your good persona, your good intentions, and feel your good vibe. You will display your love of yourself, others, life, and most importantly, the love of the Lord.

When you are able to possess these types of loves, you will inherit the powerful trait of confidence. Confidence is powerful and sexy. Confidence can be like different pieces of sexy lingerie you can wear everyday. Confidence can be the most intoxicating and alluring fragrance you can possibly wear. As a matter of fact, lightly dab some behind your earlobes right now.

Confidence can be the most comfortable pair of shoes that you can wear. When you have "on" confidence, you are all together. Now remember, in order to put confidence *on*, you must possess confidence *in* you. Wearing confidence with the love of yourself and your life along with the appreciation of even the smallest things is like being dressed sharply on a daily basis. It is similar to wearing a very nice suit with the matching hat, gloves, shoes, purse, and some very expensive jewels to top it off. Gone Girl! You look good! Nobody can't tell you nothing! Wear your confident Character in style, baby!

"RELEASE THE WEIGHTS"

You have to relax and release any traces of unforgiveness, jealousy, anger, or hatred from your being. These emotions add cracks to your foundation that will eventually become exposed. Matthews 5:43-45 says, *"love our enemies, bless those who curse you, because God does rain on the just and the unjust alike."*

So do not take the time or the energy to lash out at someone else's ignorance. Do not allow resentment to live in your Character, that is giving your power away to others. Do not let someone have power over you. Remember, do not be anyone's puppet.

"STORMS WILL COME"

When you continue to function in all areas of your life gracefully, there is no room for unnecessary weights or burdens in your life. We all go through trials and tribulations, just accept the fact that they are going to come. You have to handle them with grace. You have to remain positive.

Just say out loud right now, "storms will come into my life". Now, you have to differentiate between the storms that you bring into your life and the storms that other people may bring into your life. Either way, having the storm is not the problem; it is how you handle the storm. You can do something about it.

8 Necessities to Protect Your Character Against the Storms

1. **Your Character must have stability.**

   You need to be anchored in the areas of your life. When storms come, you cannot have a nervous breakdown. The 4 departments that make up your Character must be strong. You must have enough roots planted to remain in place. A storm should not be able to come along and just blow you all over the place. You may come through the storm a little shaken, tattered, and sometimes even a little bruised. The most important thing is that you do come through it. You are still rooted. You must remain stable.

2. **Your Character must have flexibility.**

   Sometimes when storms come, you need to adjust and readjust some areas in your life. You need to be able to do that. Sometimes you have to bob and weave, or duck and dodge. You have to be flexible to do that. You may stumble or even fall, but you need to be able to jump right back up and bounce back. Do not make permanent decisions to temporary situations. You have to be flexible.

3. **Your Character must have accountability.**

   Some storms can come from others, or our environment, but that is not always the case. You can bring storms into your own life, by the choices that you make. If you bring your own storms you must be held accountable for that. If you continue to allow the same people to bring the same storms into your life, then you must be held accountable for that, also.

4. **Your Character must have obedience.**

   When you have endured your storm and God has revealed to you what you need to do, you must be willing to obey. Your Character must have the assurance that your actions pleases God. Do not question what God has for you. You must OBEY. He will bring you through the storm. You must obey His instructions and trust His directions.

5. **Your Character must have faith, praise and worship.**

   You must praise your way through the storm. You should praise and worship the Lord no matter what storms you have and will have. You have to trust that the Lord will bring you through. No matter how bad it looks, keep praising. You can't see how He is going to do it, keep worshiping. No storm will be able to withstand *your faith, your praise, and your worship*. You have to know that what God has for you, is for you! You must always remain prayed up and allow the Holy Spirit to intercede for you. Accept God's vision for your life. Have faith in His purpose for your life.

6. **Your Character must have responsibility.**

While you are in the storm or after the storm, you must take responsibility of the lessons we have learned, and are still learning. Once you have come into the 'know', you cannot go back into the 'unknown'. You have to be responsible for you decisions and actions. There can be no more excuses. You cannot continue to look to others to blame and you must not continue to blame yourself. The storm is a lesson. It can teach you not to turn left, next time turn right. You are in charge of your destiny. You must live your Legacy. Be responsible.

7. **Your Character must have forgiveness.**

You have to be willing to forgive others for their trespasses against you. And most importantly, you must forgive yourself for any past, wrong decisions that you may have made. Forgiveness helps to cleanse your soul, renew your spirit, and remove any iniquities from your heart.

8. **Your Character must have rest.**

Your Character must be rational. Do not become so overwhelmed to the point where you do not know if you are coming or going. You must allow yourself some "down time" to rejuvenate. Allow yourself daily moments of peace. Create a quiet, peaceful, serene safe haven for yourself, even if it is only in your mind. Do not ever allow yourself to 'burn out'. You must preserve your strength for any storms. The Lord had to rest. You need to rest, also.

"HAVE FAITH"

Dr. Angela Neal-Barnett has researched the benefits of having prayer and faith in your life. Dr. Neal-Barnett found that prayer does help to heal the mind and body. There have been over 200 studies that have proven it. I absolutely agree with Dr. Neal-Barnett's observation, "Faith engenders hope, a positive element that is crucial in overcoming emotional distress."

Take every storm as a wonderful; yes *wonderful* experience to learn about yourself. Allow the storm to be an opportunity for you to grow. Let it expose things about your Character that you may have not realized before. Treat every storm as a blessing to get to know yourself better.

You can tell yourself, "I knew I was a bad sista, but I truly go it 'flat foot' going on!" Girl, be like the Timex watch, take a 'lickin' and keep on tickin'. The storms will reveal to you new strengths about yourself. You can tell yourself, "If I can handle that, I know I can handle this!" The Holy Bible tells us that life and death is in our tongues. Speak life into your Character, you can be who and whatever you say you are.

Also, while you are unveiling all these new traits and strengths about yourself, pray to have the peace of Jesus in your life. You can handle storms more effectively when you have peace. When you have the peace of Jesus in your life, your unwavering faith is your assurance that the Lord will work everything out for your good. Matthew 8:24-26, in summary, tells us that *when the storm came against the boat that Jesus and his disciples were in, He was asleep. His disciples were running around panicking and He was resting. He was resting so well to the point that they had to go and wake Him up to tell Him that they were in a storm. Jesus had to put them in check for not having any faith.*

"DO NOT STRESS"

You have to know you are going to get through your storm(s) and be determined to learn from it. Embrace your storms and be a witness to others. The very storms that use to keep you up, when you have the peace of Jesus in your life, you will be able to sleep through them. Having peace in your life is necessary.

Some things that we deem are unimaginable, you may think that you are unable to handle it, until you find yourself smack in the middle of it. Matthew 6: 26-34 in summary tells us that, *we will be taken care of by the Lord. Do not worry about Nothing! Do not worry about tomorrow, tomorrow has its own problems, take care of yourself today. God has got your back, do not stress.*

Closing Words

Accept and embrace your storms. You cannot run from your past storms. You do not want to always remain in neutral. You cannot go back and you are afraid to move forward, so you just remain in neutral. Accept your storms, face it, embrace it, get through it, and continue to move forward. Just by reading this book, I pray that you are already on your way to becoming the 'real you'.

A quote from T.S. Eliot in "Little Gidding" is;

> *We shall not cease from exploration*
> *And the end of exploring*
> *Will be to arrive where we started*
> *And know the place for the first time.*

You are forever growing. Remember, to let every situation that occurs in your life become a learning experience. You need to go back and research your foundation to see where you came from, to realize where you are going. You need to keep a journal so that you chart your journey. You will be able to see that the Lord has brought you from a mighty long way.

When you have a healthy cycle and complete balance, you will come full circle. You will know you, like it is the first time. Go ahead…meet the new you. Take yourself out, compliment yourself. Welcome truth and honesty into your life. Know that it is okay to be *Real.*

"I AM WHO I AM"

Love being Real. You do not have to get acceptance from others. When the Lord accepts you, and He does, it doesn't matter what others think. Do not waste your time trying to receive acceptance from people who do not even matter.

Luke 9: 23-25 tells us, *"If anyone desires to come after Me, let him deny himself, and take up his cross daily, and follow Me. For whoever desires to save his life will lose it, but whoever loses his life for My sake will save it. For what profit is it to a man if he gains the whole world, and is himself destroyed or lost?*

Allow the truth to live in your life. Be the 'real you' at all times. Let positive things surround you. Let positivity engulf you. Your Character needs to possess the truth. Always welcome the truth and always give the truth.

Learn to forgive others. Learn to forgive yourself. Love yourself and be available to love others. Live your life to the fullest. Find peace within yourself. Find happiness within yourself. Respect yourself and respect others. Trust your intuitions. Know the very essence of your being. Know yourself. You are who you claim yourself to be. Review your identity daily.

II Corinthians tells us, *"Behold old things are passed away. All things are become new."*

You have to be willing to embrace the truth about yourself. Know *who* you are and *whose* you. Girlfriend, you are royalty. You have a crown, place it on your head and claim your rightful place.

Accept the truth
Give the truth
Embrace the truth
Love the truth
BE THE TRUTH

In your daily walk on your self-discovery path, welcome the positivity, honesty, and truthfulness as necessary traits in your Character.

When someone asks you or if you even ask yourself, *"Who are you?"* Be confident with your response. Know exactly what you are talking about when you respond, *"I AM…"* Be as the Lord was when He answered Moses in Exodus 3:14, "I AM WHO I AM." Be exactly whoever you say you are. Love being the 'real you' at all times. ***May God Bless You and May HE continue to keep you in HIS grace.***

WHAT ARE YOUR THOUGHTS ABOUT CHAPTER 6?

WHAT HAVE YOU LEARNED FROM CHAPTER 6?

WHAT STEPS CAN YOU TAKE TO MAKE NECESSARY CHANGES IN YOUR CHARACTER FROM THE KNOWLEDGE YOU HAVE GAINED FROM CHAPTER 6?

Honestly answer these questions:

"THE NEW YOU"

1. Are you ready to make positive changes in your Character?

2. Why or why not?

3. Are you willing to be persisted until you yield the results that you want?

4. Do you feel that by reading this book that you are already on the path to positive changes in your Character?

5. How has this whole book and its exercises helped to assist you in making your transition into your Character?

6. Will you be willing to share your experiences with others?

A Final Note: It is very important to monitor your progress in your Character Journal. You need to chart your Character rebuilding process, so that you can refer back to it, so that you may see you growth pattern. Writing in your Character Journal can be very therapeutic towards becoming the 'real you', but you must be very open and very honest with yourself.

Please be Blessed and be a Blessing to someone else along your journey to finding yourself, loving yourself, living your Legacy, and becoming the 'real you' at all times.

These are a few Scriptures to help you to transform your Character. You will find what you need in the throughout the Holy Bible, but these will assist you in getting started.

CHARACTER SCRIPTURES

GENESIS 2: 2-3—And on the seventh day God ended His work which He had done, and He rested on the seventh day from all His work which He had done. Then God blessed the seventh day and sanctified it, because in it He rested from all His work which God had created and made.

JOSHUA 1:9—"Have I not commanded you? Be strong and of good courage; do not be afraid, nor be dismayed, for the Lord your God is with you wherever you go."

I SAMUEL 16:7—"But the Lord said to Samuel, "Do not look at his appearance or at his physical stature, because I have refused him. For *the Lord does not see* as man sees; for man looks at the outward appearance, but the Lord looks at the heart."

NEHEMIAH 8: 10—Then he said to them, "Go your way, eat the fat, drink the sweet, and send portions to those for whom nothing is prepared; for *this* day is holy to our Lord. Do not sorrow, for the joy of the Lord is your strength."

JOB 14:1—"Man *who* is born of woman, Is of few days and full of trouble. He comes forth like a flower and fades away; He flees like a shadow and does continue. And do You open Your eyes on such a one, And I bring me to judgment with Yourself? Who can bring a clean *thing* out of an unclean? No one!

JOB 14:7-10—"For there is hope for a tree, If it cut down, that it will sprout again, And that its tender shoots will not cease. Though its root may grow old in the earth, And its stump may die in the ground, *Yet* at the scent of water it will bud, And bring forth branches like a plant. But man dies and is laid away; Indeed he breathes his last, And where is he?

PSALM 3:3—But You, O lord, are shield for me, My glory and the One who lifts up my head. I cried to the Lord with my voice, And He heard me from His holy hill.

PSALM 4:4—Meditate within your on your bed, and be still. Offer the sacrifices of righteousness, And put your trust in the Lord.

PSALM 4:8—I will both lie down in peace, and sleep; For You alone, O Lord, make me dwell in safety.

PSALM 5:1—Give ear to my words, O lord, Consider my meditation.

PSALM 11:3—If the foundations are destroyed, What can the righteous do?

PSALM 15: 1-5—Lord, who may abide in Your tabernacle? Who may dwell in Your holy hill? He who walks uprightly, And speaks the truth in his heart; He *who* does not backbite with his tongue, Nor does evil to his neighbor, Nor does he take up a reproach against his friend; In whose eyes a vile person is despised, But he honors those who fear the Lord; He *who* swears to his own hurt and does not change; He *who* does not put out his money at usury, Nor does he take a bribe against the innocent. He who does these things shall never be moved.

PSALM 17: 3-5—You have tested my heart; You have visited *me* in the night; You have tried me and have found nothing; I have purposed that my mouth shall not transgress. Concerning the works of men, By the word of Your lips, I have kept away from the paths of the destroyer. Uphold my steps in Your paths, *That* my footsteps may not slip.

PSALM 18: 1-3—I will love You, O lord, my strength. The Lord is my rock and my fortress and my deliverer; My God, my strength, in whom I will trust; My shield and the horn of my salvation, my stronghold. I will call upon the Lord, *who is worthy* to be praised; So shall I be saved from my enemies.

PSALM 25: 4-5—Show me Your ways, O Lord; Teach me Your paths. Lead me in Your truth and teach me, For You *are* the God of my salvation; On You I wait all the day.

PSALM 25: 20-21—Keep my soul, and deliver me; Let me not ashamed, for I put my trust in You. Let integrity and uprightness preserve me, For I wait for You.

PSALM 30: 4-5—Sing praise to the Lord, you saints of His, And give thanks at the remembrance of His holy name. For His anger *is but for* a moment, His favor is *for* life; Weeping may endure for a night, But joy *comes* in the morning.

PSALM 32:5—I acknowledged my sin to You, And my iniquity I have not hidden. I said, "I will confess transgressions to the Lord," And You forgave the iniquity of my sin.

PSALM 37: 23-24—The steps of a *good* man are ordered by the Lord, And he delights in his way. Though he fall, he shall not be utterly cast down; For the Lord upholds *him with* His hand.

PSALM 38: 6-8—I am troubled, I am bowed down greatly; I go mourning all the day long. For my loins are full of inflammation, And *there* is no soundness in my flesh. I am feeble and severely broken; I groan because of the turmoil of my heart.

PSALM 38: 21-22—Do not forsake me, O Lord; O my God, be not far from me! Make haste to help me, O Lord, my salvation!

PSALM 40: 1-3—I waited patiently for the Lord; And He inclined to me, And He inclined to me, And heard my cry. He also brought me up out of a horrible pit, Out of the miry clay, And set my feet upon the rock, *And* establish my steps. He has put a new song in my mouth—Praise to our God; Many will see *it* and fear, And will trust in the Lord.

PSALM 51: 1-2—Have mercy upon me, O God, According to Your lovingkindness; According to the multitude of Your tender mercies, Blot out my transgressions. Wash me thoroughly from my iniquity, And cleanse my sin.

PSALM 51: 10-13—Create in me a clean heart, O God, And renew a steadfast spirit within me. Do not cast me away from Your presence, And do not take Your Holy Spirit from me. Restore to me the joy of Your salvation, And uphold me by *Your* generous Spirit. *Then* I will teach transgressors Your ways, And sinners shall be converted to You.

PSALM 51: 15—O Lord, open my lips, And my mouth shall show forth Your praise.

PSALM 56: 3-4—Whenever I am afraid, I will trust in You. In God (I will praise His word), In God I will put my trust; I will not fear. What can flesh do to me?

PSALM 118: 5-9—I called on the Lord in distress; The Lord answered me *and set me* in a broad place. The Lord is on my side; I will not fear. What can man do to me? The Lord is for me among those who help me: Therefore I shall see *my desire* on those who hate me. It is better to trust in the Lord, Than to put confidence in man. It is better to trust in the Lord, Than to put confidence in princes.

PSALM 118: 22-24—The stone *which* the builders rejected, Has become the chief cornerstone. This is the Lord's doing; It is marvelous in our eyes. This is the day the Lord has made; We will rejoice and be glad in it.

PSALM 121: 1-2—I will lift up my eyes to the hills—From whence comes my help? My help *comes* from the Lord, Who made heaven and earth.

PSALM 138: 1-3—I will praise You with my whole heart; Before the gods I will sing praises to You. I will worship toward Your holy temple, And praise Your name, For Your lovingkindness and Your truth; For You have magnified Your word above all Your name. In the day when I cried out, You answered me, *And* made me bold *with* strength in my soul.

PSALM 139: 1-6—O Lord, You have searched me and known *me*. You know my sitting down and my rising up; You understand my thought afar off. You comprehend my path and my lying down, And are acquainted with all my ways. For *there* is not a word on my tongue, *But* behold, O Lord, You know it altogether. You have hedged me behind and before, And laid Your hand upon me. *Such* knowledge is too wonderful for me; It is high, I cannot *attain* it.

PROVERBS 3:5-6—Trust in the Lord with all your heart, And lean not on your own understanding; In all your ways acknowledge Him, And he shall direct your paths.

PROVERBS 8: 7-11—For my mouth will speak truth; Wickedness is an abomination to my lips. All the words of my mouth *are* with righteousness; Nothing crooked or perverse is in them. They *are* all plain to him who understands, And right to those who find knowledge. Receive my instruction, and not silver, And knowledge rather than choice gold; For wisdom is better than rubies, And all the things one may desire cannot be compared with her.

PROVERBS 12: 23-27—*A prudent man conceals knowledge, But the heart of fools proclaims foolishness. The hand of the diligent will rule, But the lazy* man *will be put to forced labor. Anxiety in the heart of man causes depression, But a good word makes it glad. The righteous should choose his friends carefully, For the way of the wicked leads them astray. The lazy* man *does not roast what he took in hunting, But diligence is man's precious possession.*

PROVERBS 13:20—He who walks with wise *men* will be wise, But the companion of fools will be destroyed.

PROVERBS 13:22—A good *man* leaves an inheritance to his children's children.

PROVERBS 14:1—The wise woman builds her house, But the foolish pulls it down with her hands.

PROVERBS 16:3—Commit your works to the Lord, And your thoughts will be established.

PROVERBS 21: 2-3—Every way of a man *is* right in his own eyes, But the Lord weighs the hearts.

PROVERBS 21: 9—Better to dwell in a corner of a housetop, Than in a house shared with a contentious woman.

PROVERBS 22: 1—A good name is to be chosen rather than great riches, Loving favor rather than silver and gold.

PROVERBS 27: 17—As iron sharpens iron, So a man sharpens the countenance of his friend.

ECCLESIASTES 3:1—To everything *there* is a season, A time for every purpose under heaven.

ECCLESIASTES 3: 22—So I perceived that nothing is better than that a man should rejoice in his own works, for that is his heritage. For who can bring him to see what will happen after him?

ECCLESIASTES 5:4-5—When you make a vow to God, do not delay to pay it; For He has no pleasure in fools. Pay what you have vowed—Better not to vow than to vow and not pay.

ECCLESIASTES 11: 9-10—Rejoice, O young man, in your youth, And let your heart cheer you in the days of your youth; Walk in the ways of your heart, And in the sight of your eyes; But know that for all these God will bring you into judgment. Therefore remove sorrow from your heart, And put away evil from your flesh, For childhood and youth *are* vanity.

ECCLESIASTES 12: 13-14—Fear God and keep His commandments, For this is man's all. For God will bring every work into judgment, Including every secret thing, Whether good or evil.

ISAIAH 40: 28-31—Have you not known? Have you not heard? The everlasting God, the Lord, The Creator of the ends of the earth, Neither faints nor is weary, His understanding is unsearchable. He gives power to the weak, And to *those who have* no might He increases strength. Even the youths shall faint and be weary, And the young men shall utterly fall, But those who wait on the Lord, Shall renew *their* strength; They shall mount up with wings like eagles, They shall run and not be weary, They shall walk and not faint.

ISAIAH 61: 10—I will greatly rejoice in the Lord, My soul shall be joyful in my God; For He has clothed me with the garments of salvation, He has covered me with the robe of righteousness, As a bridegroom decks *himself* with ornaments, And as a bride adorns *herself* with her jewels. For as the earth brings forth its bud, As the garden causes the things that are sown in it to spring forth, So the Lord God will cause righteousness and praise to spring forth before all the nations.

JEREMIAH 29: 11-13—For I know the thoughts that I think toward you, says the Lord, thoughts of peace and not evil, to give you a future and hope. Then you will call upon Me and go and pray to Me, and I will listen to you. And you will seek Me and find Me, when you search for Me with all your heart.

EZEKIEL 18: 31-32—"Cast away from you all the transgressions which you have committed, and get yourselves a new heart and a new spirit. For why should you die, O house of Israel?" "For I have no pleasure in death of one who dies," says the Lord God. "Therefore turn and live!"

MATTHEW 5: 16—"Let your light so shine before men, that they may see your good works and glorify your Father in heaven."

MATTHEW 6: 24-34—"No one can serve two masters; for either he will hate one and love the other, or else he will be loyal to the one and despise the other. You cannot serve God and mammon. Therefore I say unto you, do not worry about your life, what you will eat or what you will drink; nor about your body, what you will put on. Is not life more than food and the body more than clothing? Look at the birds of the air, for they neither sow nor reap nor gather into barns; yet your heavenly Father feeds them. Are you not of more value than they? Which of you by worrying can add one cubit to his stature? So why do you worry about clothing? Consider the lilies of the field, how they grow: they neither toil nor spin; and yet I say to you that even Solomon in all his glory was not arrayed like one of these."

"Now if God so clothes the grass of the field, which today is, and tomorrow is thrown into the oven, *will He* not much more clothe you, O you of little faith? Therefore do not worry, saying, 'What shall we eat?' or 'What shall we drink?' or 'What shall we wear?' For after all these things the Gentiles seek, For your heavenly Father knows that you need all these things. But seek first the kingdom of God and His righteousness, and all these things shall be added to you. Therefore do not worry about tomorrow, for tomorrow will worry about its own things. Sufficient for the day is its own trouble.

MATTHEW 7: 1-5—"Judge not, that you be not judged. For with what judgment you judge, you will be judged; and with the measure you use, it will be measured back to you. And why do you look at the speck in your brother's eye, but do not consider the plank in your own eye? Or how can you say to your brother, 'Let me remove the speck from your eye'; and look, a plank is in your own eye?"

"Hypocrite! First remove the plank from your own eye, and then you will see clearly to remove the speck from your brother's eye."

MATTHEW 7: 7-8—"Ask, and it will be given to you; seek, and you will find; knock, and it will be opened to you. For everyone who asks receives, and he who seeks finds, and to him who knocks it will be opened."

MATTHEW 19: 26—"With men this is impossible, but with God all things are possible."

MARK 11: 22-26—"Have faith in God. For assuredly, I say to you, whoever says to this mountain, 'Be removed and be cast into the sea,' and does not doubt in his heart, but believes that those things he says will be done, he will have whatever he says. Therefore I say to you, whatever things you ask when you pray, believe that you receive *them,* and you will have *them.* And whenever you stand praying, if you have anything against anyone, forgive him, that your Father in heaven may also forgive you your trespasses. But if you do not forgive, neither will your Father in heaven forgive your trespasses."

MARK 12: 30-31—"And you shall love the Lord your God with all your heart, with all your soul, with all your mind, and with all your strength. This is the first commandment. And the second, like it, is this: 'You shall love your neighbor as yourself'. There is no other commandment greater than these."

LUKE 6: 39-40—"Can the blind lead the blind? Will they not both fall into the ditch? A disciple is not above his teacher, but everyone who is perfectly trained will be like his teacher."

LUKE 6: 43-49—"For a good tree does not bear bad fruit, nor does a bad tree bear good fruit. For every tree is known by its own fruit. For *men* do not gather figs from thorns, nor do they gather grapes from a bramble bush. A good man out of the good treasure of his heart brings forth good; and an evil man out of the evil treasure of his heart brings forth evil. For out of the abundance of the heart his mouth speaks. But why do you call Me 'Lord, Lord,' and not do the things which I say? Whoever comes to Me, and hears

My sayings and does them, I will show you whom he is like: He is like a man building a house, who dug deep and laid the foundation on the rock. And when the flood arose, the stream beat vehemently against that house, and could not shake it, for it was founded on the rock. But he who heard and did nothing is like a man who built a house on the earth without a foundation, against which the stream beat vehemently; and immediately it fell. And ruin of that house was great."

LUKE 11: 28—"Blessed *are* those who hear the word of God and keep it!"

JOHN 3-5-7—"Most assuredly, I say to you, unless one is born of water and the Spirit, he cannot enter the kingdom of God. That which is born of flesh is flesh, and that which is born of Spirit is spirit. Do not marvel that I said to you, 'You must be born again."

JOHN 3: 15—Whoever believes in Him should not perish but have eternal life.

JOHN 4: 10—"If you knew the gift of God, and who it is who says to you, 'Give Me a drink,' you would have asked Him, and He would have given you living water."

JOHN 4: 13-14—"Whoever drinks of this water will thirst again, but whoever drinks of the water that I shall give him will never thirst. But the water that I shall give him will become in him a foundation of water springing up into everlasting life."

JOHN 4:21-24—"Woman, believe Me, the hour is coming when you will neither on this mountain, nor in Jerusalem, worship the Father. You worship what you do not know; we know what we worship, for salvation is of the Jews. But the hour is coming, and now is, when the true worshipers will worship the Father in spirit and truth; for the Father is seeking such to worship Him. God is Spirit, and those who worship Him must worship in spirit and truth."

JOHN 15: 4-8—"Abide in Me, and I in you, As the branch cannot bear fruit of itself, unless it abides in the vine, neither can you, unless you abide in Me. I am the vine, you *are* the branches. He who abides in Me, and I in him, bears much fruit; for without Me you can do nothing. If anyone does not abide in Me, he is cast out as a branch and is withered; and they gather them and throw *them* into the fire, and they are burned.

If you abide in Me, and My words abide in you, you will ask what you desire, and it shall be done for you. By this My Father is glorified, that you bear much fruit; so you will be My disciples.

JOHN 16: 32-33—*"Indeed the hour is coming, yes, has now come, that you will be scattered, each to his own, and will leave Me alone. And yet I am not alone, because the Father is with Me. These things I have spoken to you, that in Me you may have peace. In the world you will have tribulation; but be of good cheer, I have overcome the world."*

ROMANS 8: 22-28—For we know that the whole creation groans and labors with birth pangs together until now. Not only *that*, but we also who have the firstfruits of the Spirit, even we ourselves groan within ourselves, eagerly waiting for adoption, redemption of our body. For we were saved in this hope, but hope that is seen is not hope; for why does one still hope for what he sees? But if we hope for what we do not see, we eagerly wait for *it* with perseverance.

Likewise the Spirit also helps in our weaknesses. For we do not know what we should pray for as we ought, but the Spirit Himself makes intercession for us with groanings which cannot be uttered. Now He who searches the hearts knows what the mind of the Spirit *is*, because He makes intercession for the saints according to *the will* of God. And we know that all things work together for good to those who love God, to those who are the called according to *His* purpose.

ROMANS 8: 30-31—Moreover whom He predestined, these He also called; whom He called, these He also justified; and whom He justified, these He also glorified. What then shall we say to these things? If God is for us, who *can be* against us?

ROMANS 8: 37—Yet in all these things we are more than conquerors through Him who loved us.

ROMANS 8: 39—Nor height nor depth, nor any other created thing, shall be able to separate us from the love of God which is in Christ Jesus our Lord.

ROMANS 12: 1-6—I beseech you therefore, brethren, by the mercies of God, that you present your bodies a living sacrifice, holy, acceptable to God, *which* is your reasonable service. And do not be conformed to this world, but be transformed by the renewing of your mind, that you may prove what is that good and acceptable and perfect will of God. For I say, through the grace given to me, to everyone who is among you, not to think *of himself* more highly than he ought to think, but to think soberly, as God has dealt to each one a measure of faith.

For as we have many members in one body, but all the members do not have the same function, so we, *being* many, are one body in Christ, and individually members of one another. Having then gifts differing according to the grace that is given to us, *let us use them.*

ROMANS 12: 21—Do not be overcome by evil, but overcome evil with good.

1 CORINTHIANS 3: 9-17—For we are God's fellow workers; you are God's field, *you are* God's building. According to the grace of God which was given to me, as a wise master builder I have laid the foundation, and another builds on it. But let each one take heed how he builds on it. For no other foundation can anyone lay than that which is laid, which is Jesus Christ. Now if anyone builds on this foundation *with* gold, silver, precious stones, wood, hay, straw, each one's work will become clear; for the Day will declare it, because it will be revealed by fire; and the fire will test each one's work, of what sort it is.

If anyone's work which he has built on *it* endures, he will receive a reward. If anyone's work is burned, he will suffer loss; but he himself will be saved, yet so as through fire. Do you not know that you are the temple of God and *that* the Spirit of God dwells in you? If anyone defiles the temple of God, God will destroy him. For the temple of God is holy, which *temple* you are.

1 CORINTHIANS 6: 19-20—Do you not know that your body is the temple of the Holy Spirit *who* is in you, whom you have from God, and you are not your own? For you were bought at a price; therefore glorify God in your body and in your spirit, which are God's.

GALATIANS 5: 1—*Stand fast therefore in the liberty by which Christ has made us free, and do not be entangled again with a yoke of bondage.*

GALATIANS 5: 25—*If we live in the Spirit, let us also walk in the Spirit.*

GALATIANS 6: 7-9—*Do not be deceived, God is not mocked; for whatever a man sows, that he will also reap. For he who sows to his flesh will of the flesh reap corruption, but he who sows to the Spirit will of the Spirit reap everlasting life. And let us not grow weary while doing good, for in due season we shall reap if we do not lose heart.*

EPHESIANS 2:8-9—*For by grace you have been saved through faith, and that not of yourselves; it is the gift of God, not of works, lest anyone should boast.*

EPHESIANS 5: 8-13—For you were once darkness, but now *you are* light in the Lord. Walk as children of light (for the fruit of the Spirit is in all goodness, righteousness, and truth), finding out what is acceptable to the Lord. And have no fellowship with the unfruitful works of darkness, but rather expose *them*. For it is shameful even to speak of those things which are done by them in secret. But all things that are exposed are made manifest by the light, for whatever makes manifest is light.

PHILIPPIANS 3: 13-14—Brethren, I do not count myself to apprehended; but one thing *I do,* forgetting those things which are behind and reaching forward to those things which are ahead, I press toward the goal for the prize of the upward call of God in Christ Jesus.

COLOSSIANS 3: 2-10—Set your mind on things above, not on things on the earth. For you died, and your life is hidden with Christ in God. When Christ *who* is our life appears, then you also will appear with Him in glory. Therefore put to death your members which are on the earth: fornication, uncleanness, passion, evil desire, and covetousness, which is idolatry.

Because of these things the wrath of God is coming upon the sons of disobedience, in which you yourselves once walked when you lived in them. But now you yourselves are put off all these: anger, wrath, malice, blasphemy, filthy language out of your mouth. Do not lie to one another, since you have put off the old man with his deeds, and have put on the new *man* who is renewed in knowledge according to the image of Him who created him.

COLOSSIANS 3: 14-15—But above all these things put on love, which is the bond of perfection. And let the peace of God rule in your hearts, to which also you were called in one body; and be thankful.

1 THESSALONIANS 5: 15-23—See that no one renders evil for evil to anyone, but always pursue what is good both for yourselves and for all. Rejoice always, pray without ceasing, in everything give thanks; for this is the will of God in Christ Jesus for you. Do not quench the Spirit. Do not despise prophecies. Test all things; hold fast what is good. Abstain from every form of evil. Now may the God of peace Himself sanctify you completely; and may your whole spirit, soul, and body be preserved blameless at the coming of our Lord Jesus Christ.

1 TIMOTHY 4: 12—Let no one despise your youth, but be an example to the believers in word, in conduct, in love, in spirit, in faith, in purity.

1 TIMOTHY 4: 15—Meditate on these things; give yourself entirely to them, that your progress may be evident to all.

TITUS 3: 2-7—Speak evil of no one, to be peaceable, gentle, showing all humility to all men. For we ourselves were also once foolish, disobedient, deceived, serving various lusts and pleasures, living in malice and envy, hateful and hating one another. But when the kindness and the love of God our Savior toward man appeared, not by works of righteousness which we have done, but according to His mercy He saved us, through the washing of regeneration and renewing of the Holy Spirit, whom He poured out on us abundantly through Jesus Christ our Savior, that having been justified by His grace we should become heirs according to the hope of eternal life.

HEBREWS 4: 1-13—Therefore, since a promise remains of entering His rest, let us fear lest any of you seem to have come short of it. For indeed the gospel was preached to us as well as to them; but the word which they heard did not profit them, not being mixed with faith in those who heard *it*. For we who have believed do enter that rest, as He has said:

> "So I swore in My wrath, They shall not enter My rest,"

Although the works were finished from the foundation of the world. For He has spoken in a certain place of the seventh *day* in this way: *"And God rested on the seventh day from all His works"*; and again in this place: *"They shall not enter My rest."* Since therefore it remains that some *must* enter it, and those to whom it was first preached did not enter because of disobedience, again He designates a certain day, saying in David, *"Today,"* after such a long time, as it has been said:

"Today, if you will hear His voice, Do not harden your hearts."

For if Joshua had given them rest, then He would not afterward have spoken of another day. There remains therefore a rest for the people of God. For he who has entered His rest has himself also ceased from his works as God *did* from His. Let us therefore be diligent to enter that rest, lest anyone fall according to the same example of disobedience. For the word of God is living and powerful, and sharper than any two-edged sword, piercing even to the division of soul and spirit, and of joints and marrow, and is a discerner of the thoughts and intents of the heart. And there is no creature hidden from His sight, but all things *are* naked and open to the eyes of Him to whom we *must give* account.

HEBREWS 12: 1-2—Therefore we also, since we are surrounded by so great a cloud of witnesses, let us lay aside every weight, and the sin which so easily ensnares *us*, and let us run with endurance the race that is set before us, looking unto Jesus, the author and finisher of *our* faith, who for the joy that was set before Him endured the cross, despising the shame, and has sat down at the right hand of the throne of God.

HEBREWS 12: 11—Now no chastening seems to be joyful for the present, but painful; nevertheless, afterward it yields the peaceable fruit of righteousness to those who have been trained by it.

HEBREWS 13: 5-8—Let *your* conduct *be* without covetousness; *be* content with such things as you have. For He Himself has said, *"I will never leave you nor forsake you."* So we may boldly say:

"The Lord is my helper; I will not fear. What can man do to me?"

Remember those who rule over you, who have spoken the word of God to you, whose faith follow, considering the outcome of *their* conduct. Jesus Christ is the same yesterday, today, and forever.

JAMES 1: 5—If any of you lacks wisdom, let him ask of God, who gives to all liberally and without reproach, and it will be given to him.

JAMES 1: 18-25—Of His own will He brought us forth by the word of truth, that we might be a kind of firstfruits of His creatures. So then, my beloved brethren, let every man be swift to hear, slow to speak, slow to wrath; for the wrath of man does not produce the righteousness of God. Therefore lay aside all filthiness and overflow of wickedness, and receive with meekness the implanted word, which is able to save your souls.

But be doers of the word, and not hearers only, deceiving yourselves. For if anyone is a hearer of the word and not a doer, he is like a man observing his natural face in a mirror; for he observes himself, goes away, and immediately forgets what kind of man he was. But he who looks into the perfect law of liberty and continues *in it,* and is not a forgetful hearer but doer of the work, this one will be blessed in what he does.

JAMES 2: 17—Faith by itself, if it does not have works, is dead.

JAMES 3: 18—Now the fruit of righteousness is sown in peace by those who make peace.

1 PETER 5: 6-7—Therefore humble yourselves under the mighty hand of God, that He may exalt you in due time, casting all your care upon Him, for He cares for you.

2 PETER 1: 2-3—Grace and peace be multiplied to you in the knowledge of God and of Jesus our Lord, as His divine power has given to us all things that *pertain* to life and godliness, through the knowledge of Him who called us by glory and virtue.

2 PETER 1: 5-8—Giving all diligence, add to your faith virtue, to virtue knowledge, to knowledge self-control, to self-control perseverance, to perseverance godliness, to godliness brotherly kindness, and to brotherly kindness love. For if these things are yours and abound, *you will be* neither barren nor unfruitful in knowledge of our Lord Jesus Christ.

CHARACTER DEFINITIONS

These definitions were retrieved from the Webster Dictionary. These are some key terms and their meanings to help assist you while you are on your path to rebuilding your Character.

I am sure there are many more, but these terms and definitions are a general overview to help define some aspects of the traits that should or should not be in your Character. Please, be Blessed along your journey.

DEFINITIONS

1. <u>Character</u>—A quality or trait that distinguishes an individual or group; a distinctive quality or trait; Distinctive; Peculiar.

2. <u>Control</u>—To have the authority or ability to regulate, direct, or dominate a situation or person.

3. <u>Alone</u>—Away from other people; simple, solitary; excluding anyone or Anything else; with nothing; sole; unaccompanied by others.

4. <u>Depth</u>—The degree or state of being deep; the distance or extent backward, downward, of inward; the most intense part of something, intensity or richness of sound or color; the range of one's comprehension.

5. <u>Along</u>—In a line with; following the length or path; in association; together; as a companion.

6. <u>Depths</u>—A deep part or place; an intense state of feeling or being.

7. <u>Empty</u>—containing nothing; vacant, lacking substance. To empty.

8. <u>Empty-Handed</u>—Having nothing in the hands.

9. <u>Empty-Hearted</u>—Having nothing in the hearts.

10. <u>Grace</u>—Seemingly effortless beauty, ease, and charm of movement, Proportion, or form; a charming quality; an attractive characteristic.

11. <u>Compathy</u>—Feelings of grief or joy shared with another.

12. <u>Emotion</u>—A strong surge of feeling; any of the feelings of fear, sorrow, joy, hate, or love; physical and psychological reaction to feelings.

13. <u>Foundation</u>—The act of founding or establishing; the basis on which anything is founded; an institution supported by an endowment; a cosmetic base for make up.

14. <u>Evolve</u>—To develop or change gradually. To be developed by evolutionary processes; to develop or work out.

15. <u>Compassion</u>—Sympathy for a person who is suffering or distressed in some way.

16. <u>Emphasis</u>—Significance of importance attached to anything.

17. <u>Forgive</u>—To pardon, to give up resentment of, to cease to feel resentment Against.

18. <u>Fulfill</u>—To convert into actually to effect; carry out; to satisfy.

19. <u>Empathize</u>—To regard with empathy.

20. <u>Forgo</u>—To give up or refrain from.

21. <u>Gracious</u>—Marked by having or showing kindness and courtesy; full of compassion; merciful.

22. <u>Inner</u>—Situated at occurring farther inside; relating to or of the mind, spirit; internal.

23. <u>Forgiving</u>—Disposed to forgive; inclined to overlook offenses; compassionate.

24. <u>Love</u>—Intense affection for another arising out of kinship or personal ties; a strong feeling of attraction resulting from sexual desire; enthusiasm or fondness.

25. <u>Relief</u>—Anything which decreases or lessens anxiety, pain, discomfort, or unpleasant conditions or feelings.

26. <u>Being</u>—One's existence.

27. <u>I</u>—The self; the ego.

28. <u>Us</u>—The objective case of we; used as an indirect object, or object of preposition.

29. <u>Relinquish</u>—To release something or someone; withdraw from; to give up.

30. <u>Relieve</u>—To lessen or ease pain, anxiety, embarrassment, or other problems; to release or free from a duty by providing a replacement.

31. <u>Search</u>—to look over carefully; to find something; to probe.

32. <u>Perserve</u>—To persist in any purpose or idea; to strive in spite of difficulties or obstacles.

33. <u>Removed</u>—State of being separate from others.

34. <u>Removable</u>—Being able to be removed.

35. <u>Remorse</u>—Deep moral regret for past misdeeds.

36. <u>Overwhelm</u>—To overcome completely; to make helpless.

37. <u>Self</u>—The complete and essential being of a person; personal interest, advantage or welfare.

38. <u>Esteem</u>—To regard with respect.

39. <u>Relive</u>—To experience something again in the imagination or fantasy.

40. <u>Spiritual</u>—Of like, or pertaining to the nature of spirit; relating to religion; Scared. Spirituality.

41. <u>Spirit</u>—The vital essence of man, considered divine in origin; the part of a human being, being characterized by personality and self conscious-

ness; the mind, The Holy Ghost; a supernatural being, as a ghost or an angel.

42. <u>GOD</u>—The Supreme Being; the ruler of life and the universe.

43. <u>Soul</u>—The spirit in the mind that is believed to be separate from the body and is the source of a person's emotional, spiritual, and moral nature.

44. <u>Persist</u>—To continue firmly despite obstacles; to endure.

45. <u>Remonstrate</u>—Giving strong reasons against an act or idea.

46. <u>Render</u>—To give or make something available; to submit or give; to represent artistically.

47. <u>Person</u>—A human being; an individual; the personality of human being.

48. <u>Personal</u>—Belonging to a person or persons; of the body or person; relating to oneself; done by yourself.

49. <u>Loner</u>—A person who avoids company of others.

50. <u>Overcome</u>—To prevail; to conquer or defeat.

51. <u>Lonely</u>—Being without companions; dejected from being alone.

52. <u>Personify</u>—To think of or represent as having human qualities or life; to be a symbol of.

53. <u>Detach</u>—To unfasten, disconnect, or separate to extricate oneself; to withdraw.

54. <u>Detract</u>—To take away from; to diminish; to divert.

55. <u>Remarkable</u>—Extraordinary.

56. <u>Remain</u>—To continue without change; to stay after the departure of others.

57. <u>Discipline</u>—Training which corrects, molds, or perfects the mental faculties or mental faculties or moral character.

58. <u>Legacy</u>—Anything that is handed down from an ancestor, predecessor, or earlier era.

59. <u>Purpose</u>—A desired goal; an intention.

60. <u>Discern</u>—To detect differences visually or with other senses or the intellect; to perceive, separate, and distinct.

61. <u>Lend</u>—To allow the temporary use or possession of something with the understanding that it is to be returned; to offer oneself as to a specific purpose.

62. <u>Purify</u>—To make clean or pure.

63. <u>Directed</u>—Guided; controlled; supervised.

64. <u>Purge</u>—To make clean; to free from guilt or sin; to rid of anything undesirable; as unwanted persons.

65. <u>Rely</u>—To trust or depend; to have confidence in someone.

66. <u>Percept</u>—A mental impression of something perceived; the immediate knowledge obtained from perceiving.

67. <u>Choice</u>—To select or choose; the opportunity, right, or power to choose.

68. <u>Private</u>—Secluded or removed from the public view; secret; intimate.

69. <u>Priority</u>—Something which takes precedence, something which be done or taken care of first.

70. <u>Final</u>—Pertaining to or coming to the end; last or terminal.

71. <u>Find</u>—To come upon unexpectedly; to achieve; to attain; to ascertain; to determine; to consider; to regard; to recover or regain something; to detect the true identity or nature of something or someone.

72. <u>Perform</u>—To execute or carry out an action; to act or function in a certain way; to act.

73. <u>Mistake</u>—A wrong statement, action, or decision.

74. <u>Change</u>—To become or make different, to alter, to put with another; to use to take place of another.

75. <u>Yesterday</u>—The day before today.

76. <u>Future</u>—The time is yet to come; a prospective condition regarding advancement or success; the future tense.

77. <u>Privilege</u>—A special right or benefit granted to a person.

78. <u>Process</u>—The course, steps, or methods toward a desired result.

79. <u>Changeable</u>—Liable of capable to change.

80. <u>Renew</u>—To make new or nearly new by restoring; to resume.

81. <u>Prime</u>—First in importance, time, or rank.

82. <u>Permission</u>—The act of permitting something; consent.

83. <u>Permit</u>—To consent to; to allow.

84. <u>Essential</u>—Necessary; indispensable, containing of, or being an essence.

85. <u>Crack</u>—To break, snap, or split apart; to break completely without separating.

86. <u>Renovate</u>—To return or restore to a good condition.

87. <u>Essence</u>—The real nature of something; the most important element; an immaterial spirit.

88. <u>Finesse</u>—A highly refined skills; the skillful handling of a situation.

89. <u>Reorganization</u>—The process of reorganizing something.

90. <u>Yourself</u>—A form of you for emphasis.

CHARACTER DEFINITIONS

91. <u>Primary</u>—First in origin, time, series or sequence, basic, fundamental.

92. <u>Team</u>—To join or work together.

93. <u>Establish</u>—To make permanent, stable, or secure; to install; to create or find; to cause to be accepted or recognized; to prove.

94. <u>Blessed</u>—Holy; enjoying happiness.

95. <u>Bless</u>—To honor or praise, to confer prosperity or well-being.

96. <u>Repress</u>—To restrain; hold back; to remove from the conscious mind.

97. <u>Level</u>—A relative position, rank, or height on a scale; a standard position from which other heights and depths are measured.

98. <u>Repower</u>—To return power anew to something or someone.

99. <u>Storm</u>—to charge or attack with a powerful force.

100. <u>Whole</u>—Complete; having nothing missing; not divided or in pieces; a complete system or unity; everything considered.

101. <u>Stifle</u>—To suffocate; to cut off; to suppress; to keep back.

102. <u>Liable</u>—Legally or rightly responsible.

103. <u>Still</u>—Silent; calm; peaceful; until now or another time. Nevertheless.

104. <u>Deposit</u>—To put, place, or set something down.

105. <u>Seek</u>—To search for; to try to research; to attempt.

106. <u>Obey</u>—To carry out instructions; to be guided or controlled; to follow directions.

107. <u>Obedient</u>—Obeying or willing to do what one is told.

108. <u>Thanks</u>—An expression of one's gratitude.

109. <u>Who</u>—Which or what certain individual, person or group.

110. <u>Confidence</u>—A feeling of self-assurance; a feeling of trust in a person; reliance; good faith.

111. <u>Secure</u>—Safe and free from doubt or fear, sturdy strong; not likely to fail.

112. <u>Repent</u>—To fell regret for something which has occurred; to change one's sinful way.

113. <u>Repair</u>—To restore to good or usable condition; to renew; to refresh.

114. <u>Celebration</u>—The act of celebrating; to demonstrate satisfaction in a festive way.

115. <u>Honesty</u>—The quality of being honest; free from deceit or fraud; straightforwardness.

116. <u>Possible</u>—Capable of being true, happening or being accomplished.

117. <u>Issues</u>—A matter of importance to solve.

118. <u>Childhood</u>—The time or period of being a child.

119. <u>Holy</u>—Regarded as having divine power; scared; spiritually pure.

120. <u>Pain</u>—Any distress or suffering of the mind; sorrow. To cause or experience pain.

121. <u>Yearn</u>—To feel a strong craving.

122. <u>Truth</u>—The facts corresponding with actual events or happenings; sincerely or honesty.

123. <u>Complete</u>—Having all the necessary parts; whole; concluded.

124. <u>Relaxed</u>—Being at rest or ease.

125. <u>Wisdom</u>—The ability to understand what is right, true or enduring; good judgment; knowledge.

126. <u>Real</u>—Something which is existing, genuine, true or authentic.

127. <u>Faith</u>—A belief in the value, truth, or trust worthiness of someone or something; belief and trust in GOD. The scriptures, or other religious writings; a system of religious beliefs.

128. <u>Commitment</u>—The act of committing; the agreement to do something in the future.

129. <u>Realize</u>—To understand correctly; to make real, to make or cause to seem real.

130. <u>Hope</u>—To want or wish for something with a feeling of confident expectation, to continue hoping for something even when it appears hopeless.

131. <u>Fake</u>—Having a false or misleading appearance; not genuine.

132. <u>Communicate</u>—To make known; to cause others to partake or share something.

133. <u>Realm</u>—A scope or field of power or influence.

134. <u>Pursue</u>—To seek; to achieve; to follow in attempt to capture.

135. <u>Action</u>—The process of doing or acting; an effect produced by something.

136. <u>External</u>—Acting from the outside; exterior.

137. <u>Joy</u>—A strong feeling of great happiness; delight. A stake or source of contentment or satisfaction; anything which makes one delighted or happy.

138. <u>Vision</u>—The power of sight; the ability to see; a supernatural appearance.

139. <u>Recognize</u>—To experience or identity something or someone as having known previously; to be appreciative.

140. <u>Patient</u>—Demonstrating uncomplaining endurance under distress.

141. <u>Heal</u>—To restore to good health, to mend the body.

142. <u>Void</u>—Containing nothing; empty; not inhabited unless; vain; without legal force or effect; null. Empty space; the quality or state of being lonely.

143. <u>Pray</u>—To address prayers to God, to ask or request.

144. <u>Worship</u>—High esteem or devotion for a person; to revere.

145. <u>Now</u>—At the present time; immediately.

146. <u>Today</u>—On or during the present day. The present time, period, or day.

147. <u>Affirm</u>—To declare positively and be willing to stand by the truth.

148. <u>Healthy</u>—In a state of or having good health; characteristic of a sound condition.

149. <u>Internal</u>—Of or pertaining to the inside, intended to be consumed by the body from the inside.

150. <u>Praise</u>—To express approval; to glorify.

151. <u>Peace</u>—A state of physical or mental tranquility; calm; serenity; the absence of war; the state of harmony between people.

152. <u>Reconstruct</u>—To build something again.

153. <u>Trait</u>—A special feature or quality of one's character.

154. <u>Journal</u>—A diary or personal daily record of observations and experiences.

155. <u>Destiny</u>—The inevitable fate to which a person or thing is destined; fate; a predetermined course of events.

156. <u>Destroy</u>—To ruin; to tear down; to demolish; to kill; to make useless or ineffective.

157. <u>Destine</u>—To be determined in advance to design or appoint a distinct purpose.

158. <u>Pertain</u>—To relate to; to refer to; to belong as a function, adjunct or quality, to appreciate or fitting.

159. <u>Accept</u>—To take what is given to believe to be true; to agree; to receive something.

160. <u>Press</u>—To act upon or exert steady pressure or force.

161. <u>Stop</u>—To cease; to halt; to refrain from moving, operating, or acting.

162. <u>Will</u>—The mental ability to decide or choose for oneself, strong desire or determination.

163. <u>Destructible</u>—Capable of being destroyed.

164. <u>Determination</u>—The act of deciding definitely; a firm resolution; adherence to purpose or aim.

165. <u>Enduring</u>—Lasting.

166. <u>Endure</u>—To undergo; to sustain; to put up with; to tolerate; to bear.

167. <u>Develop</u>—To bring out or expand the potentialities, to make more elaborate; to enlarge; to evolve; to advance from a lower to a higher stage from an earlier later stage of maturation.

168. <u>Unfold</u>—To reveal gradually.

169. <u>Positive</u>—Containing, expressing, or characterized by affirmation; very confident; absolutely certain; not negative.

170. <u>Destination</u>—The point or place to which something or someone is directed, the purpose or end for which something is created or intended.

171. <u>Extraordinary</u>—Beyond what is usual or common; remarkable.

172. <u>Unessential</u>—Not being important.

173. <u>Purity</u>—The quality of being pure; freedom from guilt or sin.

174. <u>Serene</u>—Calm; peaceful

175. <u>Uneasy</u>—Feeling or causing distress or discomfort; embarrassed; awkward; uncertain.

176. <u>Pleasant</u>—Giving or promoting the feeling of pleasure; very agreeable.

177. <u>Travail</u>—Strenuous material physical exertion; to undergo the sudden sharp pain of childbirth.

178. <u>Unforeseen</u>—Not anticipated or expected.

179. <u>Plight</u>—A distressing circumstance, situation or condition.

180. <u>Reconsider</u>—To think about again with a view to changing a previous action or decision.

181. <u>Rejoice</u>—To fill with joy; to be filled with joy.

182. <u>Contemplate</u>—To look over; to ponder; to consider thoughtfully.

183. <u>Reinstate</u>—To restore something to its former position or condition.

184. <u>Humble</u>—Marked by meekness or modesty, unpretentious.

185. <u>Reciprocation</u>—A mutual exchange; an alternating motion.

186. <u>Pliable</u>—Flexible; easily controlled or persuaded.

187. <u>Reinvigorate</u>—To restore vigor.

188. <u>Exalt</u>—To raise in character, honor, rank, etc. To praise or glorify; to increase the intensity of someone or thing.

189. <u>Conscience</u>—The ability to recognize right and wrong regarding <u>one's</u> own behavior.

190. <u>Obligation</u>—A promise or feeling or duty; something one must do because of one's conscience or law demands it.

191. <u>Recipient</u>—A person who receives.

192. <u>Broken-down</u>—Shattered or collapsed; ruined.

193. <u>Abundantly</u>—Plentiful; sufficient degree; ample; plentifully.

194. <u>Objective</u>—Something that owe works toward, a goal; a purpose.

195. <u>Reconstruction</u>—Something which has been reconstructed or rebuilt.

196. <u>Recovery</u>—The power to regain something.

197. <u>Wail</u>—A loud, mournful cry or weep. To make such a sound.

198. <u>Justify</u>—To be just; right, or valid; to declare guiltless.

199. <u>Evidence</u>—Signs or facts on which a conclusion can be based; that which makes evident or indication of something.

200. <u>Pride</u>—A sense of personal dignity; a feeling of pleasure because of something achieved, alone, or owned.

201. <u>Hopeful</u>—Manifesting or full of hope.

202. <u>Honor</u>—High regard or respect, personal integrity reputation; privilege. To accept something as valid; to treat with respect.

203. <u>Courage</u>—Mental or moral strength to face danger (challenge).

204. <u>Calm</u>—Absence of motion, having little or rewind, storms, or rough water.

205. <u>Evident</u>—Easily understood or seen; obvious.

206. <u>Comfort</u>—To make someone feel better; to help; to assist, to have relief or satisfaction; solace.

207. <u>Barter</u>—To trade something for something else without the exchange of money; one commodity for another.

208. <u>Clarify</u>—To become or make clearer.

209. <u>Mannerism</u>—A person's distinctive behavioral trait or traits.

210. <u>Bargain</u>—To negotiate over price, (worth) of something (someone).

211. <u>Habits</u>—Involuntary pattern of behavior acquires by frequent repetition; manner of conducting oneself.

212. <u>Epitomize</u>—To serve as a perfect example.

213. <u>Give</u>—To donate or contribute; to apply; to devote.

214. <u>Laugh</u>—To express or show joy, merriment or amusement.

215. <u>Image</u>—A representation of the form and features of someone or something.

216. <u>Energy</u>—Vigor; strength; capacity or tendency for working or acting; vitality of expression.

217. <u>Give-and-Take</u>—To make a mutual exchange.

218. <u>Origin</u>—The cause or beginning of something; the source; a beginning place.

219. <u>Enthusiast</u>—A person full of enthusiasm for something.

220. <u>Privilege</u>—A special right or benefit granted to a person.

221. <u>Respect</u>—To show consideration or esteem for; to relate to; courtesy or considerate treatment.

222. <u>Entity</u>—The fact of real existence; something that exist alone.

223. <u>Deserve</u>—To be worthy of or entitled to.

224. <u>Metamorphosis</u>—The transformation and change in the structure and habits.

225. <u>Encourage</u>—To inspire with courage or hope; to support.

226. <u>Secure</u>—Safe and free from doubt or fear; sturdy or strong; not likely to fail.

227. <u>Kneel</u>—To get down upon one's knees.

228. <u>Social</u>—Having to do with people living in groups; enjoying friendly companionship with others.

"Beware of your thoughts, they become words.
Beware of your words, they become actions."
Beware of your actions, they become habits.
Beware of your habits, they become Character.
Beware of your Character, it will become your destiny."

—Frank Outlaw

ABOUT THE AUTHOR

Keke M. Robinson is a Christian, who is very grateful to the Lord for His second and third chances. She is President and CEO of CHARACTER Consulting Services. She is an educator, motivational speaker, consultant, advisor, and a poet. Her "down-home" style of teaching is similar to having an intimate conversation with friends. She is a widely sought after speaker. She is a firm believer in building Character. She is dedicated to spreading the gospel of Jesus Christ worldwide. She possesses a Bachelor of Arts degree from the University of Arkansas-Monticello. She and her family resides in Georgia.

0-595-32780-X

Printed in the United States
25603LVS00004B/445-504